Cherry Hill

Raising Successful Black Children in Jim Crow Baltimore

Linda G. Morris

ISBN 9781940773476

For purposes of bulk purchase contact
History Publishing Media Group LLC
Historypublish@aol.com

SAN: 850-5942

First Edition

Published by History Publishing Company Global an imprint of History Publishing Media Group LLC, Palisades, NY 10964.

"This book is dedicated to our parents who had the courage to be pioneers, the vision to see the potential for a wasteland, and the faith to bring us on an awesome journey."

Foreword

I moved to Baltimore from Buffalo, New York, circa 1964 when I was 10 years old during the beginning of President Lyndon Johnson's Great Society. We moved to the Forest Park neighborhood which, at that time, was the premier area of northwest Baltimore for black families. My circle was a closed one consisting of family, church folks, and neighborhood friends. It was a Norman Rockwell setting of large frame houses inhabited by physicians, judges, lawyers, and ministers. There were churches on every corner and having been raised as a preacher's daughter, it was expected that life center around the church. We had large backyards with apple and pear trees, and every family had an automobile—preferably, as my family did—a Cadillac.

The first time I ever met anyone from Cherry Hill was when I entered Northwestern High School. The furthest south I had ever ventured in Baltimore City was Hilton Street. When I heard the name, Cherry Hill, I envisioned hills sprinkled with cherries. I just knew these classmates chose to come to this predominantly Jewish high school from somewhere in Baltimore City that was unfamiliar to me, and that I had no reason to get to know them.

Fast forward to March 2014 when I had the opportunity to go to Cherry Hill. I was administering testing to elementary school children, and I got lost on my first attempt to find it. Cherry Hill is tucked away on a peninsula with only two entrances—one on each end of the community. As soon as I turned off of Waterview Road onto Cherry Hill Road, I felt as though I had left Baltimore City and stumbled into the country. There was an unsightly commercial area that led to the "town." There were old brick row homes, which I later found out were projects, high on a hill to my right with old boarded up single family homes to my left. As I drove around to find the school, there was a juxtaposition of old and new structures with no rhyme or reason. There was a large central section of two-story small brick row houses—more projects—that were painted a drab dark red, and they looked like a prison camp. When I finally arrived at the school, it was a dreary, stark monumental structure that looked more like a penal institution than an environment for learning. As I entered the school, I was hit by the sight and smell of feces which the janitor mopped up as students walked by holding their noses. This, I thought, is *Cherry Hill?*

Needless to say, I was not impressed. I was in fact horrified. It must have shown because one of my colleagues, Sandra Green Johnson, said she had grown up here along with a mutual friend, Linda Morris, and that they loved Cherry Hill. Sandra said, "I'm going to tell Linda that you don't like Cherry Hill." She did, and that's how this whole project got started. This book is an effort to convince me that Cherry Hill was, is, and shall be again, a great place to live.

Cherry Hill sits on and overlooks Baltimore's Inner Harbor. Kevin Plank, the CEO of Under Armour is courting the City for a loan to let him redevelop the waterfront from Westport to Port Covington, the section of the Harbor adjacent to Cherry Hill. Maybe, just maybe, there will be something in that deal that will cause Cherry Hill to shake off the ashes under which it finds itself and rise like the Phoenix it could become. Rising with the hopes and dreams of families and inspiration for Cherry Hill's children—with a few cherries on top.

Sherrie Davis, MHS

1.

N.I.M.B.Y. (Not In My Back Yard)!

Before Opie lived in Mayberry, Beaver and Wally in Mayfield, and Betty, Bud and Kathy in Springfield, there were thousands of little Black children experiencing the same quality of life in Cherry Hill, a post WWII planned suburban community containing a public housing project on a southeastern peninsula of Baltimore City. These children had a sense of being loved, being free, being safe, and above all, having the space they needed to stretch out and enjoy small town living. They could play all day with their friends, skate and ride their bikes all over town, and chase the ice cream man's truck, with the admonishment to be home by the time the streetlights came on. I should know. I was one of these children, and I have rallied sixty or so of my Cherry Hill contemporaries to share what life was like for us in what we know to be a special place and time.

Our families moved to Cherry Hill because it was a chance to leave the run-down, second-hand housing of Baltimore's inner city and live in brand new homes created just for us. Cherry Hill, separated from the rest of Baltimore by train tracks to the north, the Middle Branch of the Patapsco River to the east, and the Hanover Street Bridge to the south, offered isolation and freedom from the rigors of living in tight and over-populated city street grids. It also offered the opportunity to shape and mold a lifestyle on par with other planned communities of the time.

Some families were recruited because they had someone working in the defense industry that was important to the WWII war effort. Others were in need of affordable housing in a very segregated Baltimore City that stifled their mobility with housing covenants that kept them in the deteriorating structures of the inner city. Still, by the time the community was actually built and families began moving in, others had veterans returning from a war in which they were good enough to fight, but not good enough to choose any neighborhood in Baltimore to find a decent place to call home.

What a wondrous place Cherry Hill was—planned with everything the community needed to support self-sufficiency—schools, churches, a community center, a shopping center, a public swimming pool, and neighborhood playgrounds and parks. We had our medical clinics staffed by doctors who lived in the community. We even had our own bus number, 37. The only place the 37 went was to Cherry Hill, so even if you couldn't read, you knew that number and what it meant. The bus leaving Cherry Hill was the 28. The 28 and 37 ran parallel routes coming back toward Cherry Hill, but that route separated when you got to Westport, a white community adjoining Cherry Hill. The number 37 signaled that the bus was full of black people going to a black neighborhood. We didn't object because we just went about the business of living and shaping life in Cherry Hill.

Cherry Hill was lush with vegetation not seen in the city. There were apple, crab apple, peach, plum, fig, and pear trees, raspberries, grapes, and black rum cherries, the cherries for which Cherry Hill was named. There were also plenty of mint bushes and honeysuckle vines that kept the air so fragrant, and that's important when your community is built next to a trash dump and incinerator. Actually, because of its water front location and lush foliage, Cherry Hill was seriously considered as a site for a major City park. In 1905, the Olmsted Brothers, the Massachusetts landscape architects who designed New York's Central Park, presented a report recommending that the site be developed as a public park. When J. Wilson Leakin, a prominent Baltimore lawyer, died in 1922, he bequeathed the city property to sell—which was later sold for $145,000—for the purpose of developing a park for the people of the City.

The battle as to where to locate the J. Wilson Leakin Memorial Park went on for about 17 years. Finally, in 1940, the Brooklyn Board of Trade approached the Baltimore City Council to implement the recommendation of the Olmstead Report and to also include a cross-town connection to create a by-pass from south to west Baltimore which would relieve traffic coming out of Brooklyn crossing the Hanover Street Bridge. The owners of the 52 acres of the Cherry Hill property containing the waterfront offered the City the land for $140,000—which the City considered high. The other site in contention was a parcel of property located in the Crimea estate along Franklintown Road in southwest Baltimore. In

January 1940, the City Council committee on parks voted to put Leakin Park on the Cherry Hill site because they felt that it was more accessible to the people than the Crimea estate site. However, by June 1940 the full Council vote selected the Crimea estate along Franklintown Road as the Leakin Park site.

At the time it was being developed for housing and into the early 1960s, the signature gateway to Cherry Hill when making the right turn from Waterview Avenue onto Cherry Hill Road (one of only two entrances into the development) were these magnificent high terra cotta red clay wooded cliffs. They looked so other worldly that you knew this had to be a special place. That red soil, rich in iron content, provided a means of support for the early colonists who arrived from England and mined the iron and helped to establish Baltimore's industrial prowess. From the middle of the 19th century, Cherry Hill had earned a very exotic reputation. Its fertile soil and forestation had been the home of farmers, secret societies, and amusement parks and resorts for "colored" folks. In the early 1900s, the DuPont Powder Company of Delaware, forerunner to the DuPont Chemical Company, owned a 35-acre farm in Cherry Hill that stored 10,000 to 20,000 pounds of dynamite and powder, used for agriculture and war, enough to blow up the city. It was such a dangerous installation that the company employed a couple to keep hunters from shooting near the dynamite magazine.

All this is to say, Cherry Hill was no run-of-the-mill place. While Cherry Hill was a wonderful home town for us, had it not been for President Franklin Roosevelt's New Deal and all the accompanying local political wrangling of Baltimore Mayors Howard W. Jackson, Democrat, and Theodore R. McKeldin, progressive Republican, newly elected in 1943, Cherry Hill may never have happened. In his 1994 500-page John's Hopkins University dissertation thesis, Local Deals and the New Deal State: Implementing Federal Public Housing in Baltimore 1933 to 1968, Peter H. Henderson lays out the battle to execute New Deal Federal housing policy locally which ultimately birthed Cherry Hill. With the tremendous work done by Henderson, the help of the historical archives of the Baltimore Sun and the Afro American newspapers, and the guidance of the librarians in the Enoch Pratt Free Library's Maryland Room, we have been able to excavate the most compelling story of how, from the ashes of man's inhumanity to his fellow man, something with measurable social significance can yet arise.

Mayor Jackson served his first term as Mayor of Baltimore from 1923 to 1927 where he was an early proponent of fairness and good schools for

Mayor Howard W. Jackson 1923-1927 and 1931-1943

blacks. He was defeated in 1927 by his predecessor, William F. Broening, a Republican, but re-elected in 1931. Mayor Jackson, an insurance executive and accountant, served three consecutive terms ending in 1943. He guided Baltimore through the depression by creating a social welfare system that got the massive unemployed and destitute population of Baltimore City through the Great Depression and is credited with keeping the city's financial rating in tact through hard times. Mayor Jackson had a comfortable relationship with Baltimore's black community and its leadership and included them in his open door policy.

In response to the economic devastation of the Great Depression, President Roosevelt put forth a slate of programs to meet the needs of the people—one of which was affordable housing. On October 27, 1937, President Roosevelt signed the Wagner-Steagall Act that created the United States Housing Authority (USHA) to oversee Federal funding for low income housing through loans and grants to local jurisdictions. Baltimore's black population was growing rapidly as the result of the in-migration of Southern blacks looking for work in the defense industry and a better life, but it was not politically active. The *Afro-American Newspaper*, founded by John H. Murphy, Sr., in 1892, championed the causes of Baltimore's black community. The Urban League formed a local chapter in Baltimore in 1925. In the mid-1930s, Mrs. Lillie Carroll Jackson became the President of the Baltimore Chapter of the National Association for the Advancement of Colored People (NAACP) with Thurgood Marshall as the chapter's attorney. It took all of these entities to speak truth to power—that Baltimore needed housing for its black citizens, and that Baltimore needed to take advantage of the Federal housing funding being offered to the nation's cities.

Mayor Jackson listened, and on December 14, 1937, he signed City Council legislation, creating the Housing Authority of Baltimore City (HABC) and proceeded to appoint its five-man Board of Commissioners. In spite of the Council's rejection of a resolution to select a black Commissioner, Mayor Jackson appointed Dr. George B. Murphy, the son of the *Afro-American Newspaper* founder, as a member of the HABC's Board of Commissioners. Dr. Murphy was the Vice Chairman of the Urban League and the retired Principal of Frederick Douglass High School, one of only two high schools for blacks in Baltimore City. Initially, the HABC put together a proposal to obtain Federal funding to demolish slum buildings and build five public housing projects, and on June 3, 1938, President Roosevelt approved a $16,616,000 loan to the HABC. This loan provided funding for Latrobe, McCulloh, Perkins, Poe, and Douglass Homes. Funding to build two vacant land sites was requested in February 1939, and the Federal loan was revised upwards for a total of $26,390,000. One site was to house white families, Armstead Gardens, and the other black families, Cherry Hill.

These projects were vigorously protested by white neighborhood associations who thought that their homes would be devalued, but once Mayor Jackson gave assurances that Armstead Gardens would only house whites, that protest stopped. Cherry Hill was another matter. White residents, mortgage bankers, and realtors vehemently protested at the April 22, 1939, Board of Estimates meeting, that the site at Cherry Hill, "would greatly depreciate the entire section and add to the traffic hazard, and that it would be dangerous for white school children and white persons going to and from work to pass through this area." On June 27, 1939, the Board of Estimates approved the Armstead Gardens site, and Armstead Gardens opened to tenants in 1941. It did not approve the Cherry Hill site forcing the HABC to withdraw it from consideration.

In the meantime, the advent of WWII complicated Federal housing policy. Baltimore was a major defense industry city. Glenn L. Martin Aircraft, the forerunner of Lockheed Martin, manufactured airplanes for the war in Middle River, an eastern suburb of the city. War ships were being built at the Sparrows Point Shipyards. Bethlehem Steel manufactured steel for both. Baltimore's labor force grew exponentially with the in-migration of white and black workers flocking to Baltimore to meet the needs of the defense industry. Although the newly built public housing developments eased the need for housing somewhat, it remained at crisis level for black defense workers. On October 14, 1940, Congress passed the Lanham Act which authorized a defense housing program and stipulated that it be administered separate and apart from the low-income housing program; and that the defense housing be only temporary. For a number of reasons, Armstead Gardens did not attract enough low-rent applicants, and the Federal Government purchased the project from the HABC for defense housing.

In March 1943, the Federal Government proposed three sites to the HABC for the development of housing for black defense industry workers, one of which was located at Eastern Avenue and Northpoint Road in Baltimore County, a white area. This site was chosen because it was close to Glenn L. Martin and Bethlehem Steel. The approval of this site became a political hot potato because by then a 1942 amendment to national housing legislation required the USHA to get approval of sites from the local jurisdiction. The Canton Railroad owned 126 acres of the 159-acre proposed site, and O. H. Nance, President of the Canton Company, objected to selling it because he knew it would lower the property values of the white home owners, and subsequently impact the price he could get for adjacent land he was trying to sell for residential construction. In addition, the Eastern Confederation of Civic Associations protested putting a black development anywhere near the homes they represented. The Chairman of the HABC did not want a temporary or permanent housing development for blacks built on vacant land anywhere.

Another site was recommended near Armstead Gardens within Baltimore City near Herring Run Park because it was "on the edge of an industrial area and well removed from any white settlement." The HABC decided to send this recommendation forward along with suggestions for other sites, one of which was Cherry Hill. Most of the HABC Board voted to approve the Cherry Hill site with the exception of Dr. Murphy, the only black Board member. Dr. Murphy, along with Mayor Jackson, and the Federal Government objected to Cherry Hill for permanent housing because it contained a city incinerator and a city-owned cemetery (a potter's field on which two schools were subsequently built), and abutted the polluted Patapsco River, marshlands, and a railroad right-of-way. They deemed it unsuitable for human habitation.

Linda G. Morris

By June 1943, the newly elected Mayor McKeldin was acutely aware of the burgeoning black housing crisis, and appointed an Inter-racial Commission of nine citizens, seven white and two black, to resolve the site issue. He also was reluctant to use the $8,000,000 from the initial USHA Loan to the HABC to build just temporary housing. The Inter-racial Commission selected the Herring Run site. The site approval caused a major uproar in the communities adjacent to and surrounding Herring Run Park.

In July, 800 white disgruntled Northeast Baltimore residents descended on the War Memorial Building to meet with the Mayor and find out who was responsible for the choice of the Herring Run site. The crowd was led by three Third District City Councilmen, two Catholic Priests, a Jewish Rabbi, and a Methodist minister. They accused the Mayor, his Inter-racial Commission, and all the agencies involved, including the Federal Housing Authority (FHA), of passing the buck to each other denying responsibility for the selection of the site The meeting got so heated that one boisterous demonstrator yelled, "To hell with the Federal Government," and the crowd began to boo the Mayor. When the Mayor got up to speak, visibly annoyed by the booing and after listening to an hour of complaints from the crowd, he told them that just as he had been courteous enough

Theodore R. McKeldin, Baltimore Mayor 1943-1947, 1963-1967

to listen to them, he expected the same courtesy from them. He let them know that if he had made the selection, he would be courageous enough to say so. He let the crowd know that he was "as much opposed to in-migrant colored workers as you are," but that they faced an acute housing problem and something had to be done about it. The general complaint was that the area was a white community and lacked the infrastructure to support and sustain the segregated way of life, i.e., schools, churches, entertainment, transportation, and water sewage. They recommended two other sites to the Mayor—Turner's Station and Cherry Hill.

At the request of those opposing the Herring Run site, the Vice President of the City Council asked the City Solicitor to write an opinion that any decision would have to come from the municipal corporation as a whole, acting through the City Council. This was such an emotionally charged political issue, the City Council didn't even vote to make a recommendation. Everyone kept passing the buck not wanting to alienate the white community by recommending a site. The Federal government then told the Mayor and City Council that "it has been determined that there is critical need in Baltimore for war housing for Negroes." The FPHA said it would "proceed with the construction of a temporary project to meet this need." Black groups became upset with the Mayor for letting this opportunity to build permanent housing for the black community slip away.

The Federal Government proceeded to work to purchase the Herring Run Site. The Mayor was looking at alternative sites in south Baltimore. There were a lot of structural and technical difficulties involved with the Cherry Hill site including a ten-inch water main that had low water pressure and no sewer line. There were no schools and no business district. Also plans for a white park would be disrupted and Broening Park, which the city had developed and due to low usage turned over to the Yacht Club, would have to be reclaimed and "converted to colored use." The up side of developing Cherry Hill was that it would adjoin another black housing project, Mt. Winans, and the entire area could be developed for the use of a large black population without overcrowding. By August 1943, two private developers had already received backing from the FHA to build private homes for sale to blacks in Cherry Hill, thus furthering the impetus to select Cherry Hill as a public housing site. The thinking was that there would be little continued public interest in the site at Cherry Hill, and therefore, the Mayor and local officials selected it and announced the selection in December.

Meanwhile, the Federal Government was proceeding with plans to acquire the Herring Run site. They asked the City to reconsider Herring Run, but the City proposed a package of three temporary sites in east Baltimore containing between 1,000-1,100 dwellings, and a permanent site in Cherry Hill—stipulating that the package had to be accepted in its entirety. The FPHA accepted the package and decided that it would build Cherry Hill because of the hostility the HABC had shown toward building permanent housing for blacks on vacant land.

There were protests from whites who lived in Brooklyn, a white south Baltimore neighborhood to the southeast of the Cherry Hill site, against building housing for blacks in Cherry Hill. The Urban League and the NAACP joined the protests because the area had industrial zoning, the site was low marsh land, a city incinerator was located there, and it was next to the Baltimore and Ohio railroad track. The Urban League predicted that, "unless the many factors involved in the Cherry Hill site are more carefully analyzed and satisfactory answers given, we may be confronted with social situations which are far more disastrous than the housing problem with which we are now confronted." The NAACP threatened to take court action to stop the development from being built on the site, but it didn't. Both groups came to the realization that for the first time in Baltimore City history, new housing was being built for blacks on vacant land—quite a coup.

2.

Birth of the Cherry Hill Plan

D. Fred Crowley, the author of a short article in a 1940 Yacht Club publication, *Kedge Anchor,* described the Cherry Hill he knew as a child. "As a schoolboy, Cherry Hill used to be our 'gang's' playground and we would go there to gather chestnuts, persimmons, magnolias, walnuts, honeysuckle, and hunt frogs. The view from the top is truly beautiful with Spring Gardens below and a near view of the City. It is positively enchanting. You have here the same height as Federal Hill, but you get a better view of the City."

The Cherry Hill of the early 1940s was heavily wooded with isolated farms, shacks, trailers, and bungalows, sprinkled throughout the area. Baltimore City acquired 275 acres of land on the Cherry Hill peninsula to develop as "Baltimore's planned community for the colored." This was the first time in the country that a city brought together private and public housing to create a new and modern community for blacks. At that time, 35 acres were cleared for the development of private residences including Cherry Hill Village, Cherry Wood, DuPont Manor, and Waterview Homes; 79 acres were cleared for Cherry Hill Homes, the public housing component. The remaining 161 acres were held for the development of parks and future expansion.

By November 1943, there was concern that construction was going on in Cherry Hill by private developers without a coordinated plan for the community and public services. Kathryn D. Barnett, Executive Secretary of the City Planning and Housing Association, and J. Harvey Kerns, Executive Secretary of the Baltimore Urban League, formed a citizens' group and issued a joint announcement asking that the Commission on City Plan produce a consolidated plan. They wrote, "It appears that the Baltimore Housing Authority is developing plans to build a permanent housing project for Negroes on a site in the Cherry Hill section. It also appears that the Baltimore Commission on City Plan is attempting to assist a number of private real estate operators who have submitted individual plans for the development of adjacent sites, in order to have the several subdivisions fit a master street and lot plan for the Cherry Hill area."

The citizens' group's concern was that if projects were undertaken individually with no commitment to a larger vision for public services, the new community, "the first effort to select and develop new areas for colored housing in Baltimore," would fail. The group wanted plans for "water, sewage disposal, drainage, schools, churches, stores, park, recreation, zoning protection from industrial encroachment, etc. to serve this area as a unit." John D. Steele, Chairman of the Commission on City Plan, refuted the allegation that there was no plan, and said that a master plan for providing public services had been worked out two months prior and had been agreed to by the builders and the FHA. Steele said that his office had begun making plans as soon as it was evident that the site would be selected. He said that preparations had been made for every public service with the exception of churches, institutions over which he had no control. Steele said that he sent the plans to the FHA, and that the FHA directed all those concerned with the Cherry Hill project to work out the details with the Commission. The Cherry Hill Plan was born and begun to be implemented.

Cherry Hill: A Community History by John R. Breihan, a professor at Baltimore's Loyola College, is a 30-page anecdotal and documentary history published in 2003. According to Dr. Breihan, the planners made a conscious decision to make Cherry Hill "a city on the hilltop." Some of the same ideas used in constructing Roland Park, Guilford, and Homeland, Baltimore's white planned suburban communities, were used to construct Cherry Hill. The planners decided to use curving streets following the natural slopes of the hillsides to emphasize nature and calm traffic since the thinking was that traffic could not travel as fast as it could on straight streets. Roundview and Bridgeview Roads formed an inner oval and Seamon and Reedbird Avenues and Round Road formed an outer oval. The remaining roads curved off of these. The community shopping center was to go in the center of the ovals at the top of the hill overlooking the harbor.

Construction began at the waterfront and worked its way up the hill. The FHA encouraged private builders to construct houses in Cherry Hill for even the lowest paid war workers by offering them low-interest loans and access to building materials left over from the war at surplus pricing. Another benefit of the construction of war housing was the work it provided for the labor force. However, just as with other facets of life in Baltimore, blacks lagged behind whites with employment. As Cherry Hill Village, the first development of private homes, was being constructed by Edward and Julius Myerberg in September 1944, Nick Campitelli, the contractor, refused to hire black brick layers. He stated that hiring "colored" workmen was against his policy because it might cause him to lose his white workers. Harry Minskoff, president of Cherry Hill Village, said that many "colored" employees, including skilled cement workers and fitters, had been used in the construction work, but it was not the policy of his company to question the hiring practices of the contractors. There were fewer than 30 black brick layers in Baltimore, and blacks were barred from union membership. In order to get work, black brick layers had to join out-of-town unions and then get a clearance from the Baltimore union to take a job. Consequently, no black brick layers worked on Cherry Hill Village.

The Baltimore Sun ran the following housing ad on September 30, 1944: IN-MIGRANT WAR WORKERS: If you have been living in Baltimore since 1941, or if you have lived in Baltimore longer and are being evicted from your home, you can rent or buy an outstanding home in beautiful Cherry Hill Village. Take No. 6 car to Cherry Hill Road and Hanover Street. Walk 2 blocks west. Furnished sample house open daily, 10:30 a.m. to 8:30 p.m.

Cherry Hill Village opened with 196 row houses for sale and rent. The inside units had two bedrooms and sold for $4,700 to $5,100, and the end units had 3 bedrooms and went for $5,300 to $5,700. Rents for the same units ranged from $46.25 to $48.25 per month. Cherry Hill Village included homes on Southland, Swale, and Seagull Avenues, Ascension Street (the only Street in Cherry Hill), and Bridgeview and Roundview Roads.

Morris and Morton Macht of the Welsh Construction Company built the Cherrywood development. Cherrywood consisted of row houses, referred to architecturally as "Venti-lite" houses, set at a 45-degree angle to the street with large windows, along Cherry Hill Road, and 163 two-family stacked apartments on Cherry Hill Road between Seamon and Southland Avenues. The apartments sold for $8,250 to $8,400 (for the two-family unit) or rented for $41.49 per month for a single unit.

Cherrywood "Venti-lite houses

DuPont Manor was the third set of private homes. It was built at the top of Cherry Hill near the future Community Building and across from the public housing to come. These homes were built by Jerome Kahn, a Pikesville architect and real estate developer, and included 152 row houses along Booker T Drive (named for Booker T. Washington) and Carver (named for Dr. George Washington Carver) and Woodview Roads. There is another group of Venti-lite houses along Woodview Road. They sold for from $4,850 to $5,400 and rented for $46.25 a month. Kahn also bought an adjacent parcel of land on which he built Waterview Homes, including Terra Firma, Cheraton and Hillview Roads in 1948. These homes were advertised for sale only in November 1948 for $7,250 with a $500 down payment.

The FPHA broke ground for Cherry Hill Homes, the public housing, in 1944. The original units were built on the northwest end of the development. One grouping of homes and apartments was built within an oval composed of Shellbanks, Berea, Slater, and Sethlow Roads. The crossroads within the oval were Giles, Fisk, and Blyden Roads. Another grouping was built along Spelman Road, with Claflin and Windwood Courts—courts being cul-de-sacs—and Denham Circle intersecting Spelman. Spelman Road ran parallel to Round Road (formerly Old Annapolis Road and renamed for J. Emory Round, the first president of Morgan State University) which was a main road through the public housing. All row housing

13

units were barracks style and had individual front yards and porches with common green areas behind them. Play areas with swings, see-saws, sliding boards, merry-go-rounds, and sand boxes, were also built in each neighborhood.

The first residents of Cherry Hill Homes did not start moving in until December 1945. Many of the streets were not paved, and sidewalks had not been laid. The street lights weren't up yet, and bus transportation was not convenient. The shopping center that would service the community was not built yet. This did not stop the influx of families into the new development. They came because it was far better than their circumstances in the inner city.

Among the first public housing residents were Shepherd and Myrtle Burge. Mr. Burge received a degree in health and physical education from the University of Arkansas at Pine Bluff where he met Mrs. Burge. After graduating, he joined the army and moved his family to Pennsylvania where he was assigned to a hospital as a nurse. After being discharged from the service, Mr. Burge was offered a job with the Department of Recreation in Baltimore. The Burges moved to Cherry Hill from Pennsylvania in 1945 with their two small children. When the Burges went to sign the papers for their public housing unit, Mrs. Burge expressed her thanks to the manager of Cherry Hill Homes, Mr. Otho Pinkett, for being selected to live in the new community. She told him how they had lived in a 3rd floor apartment when they first got to Baltimore, and how hard it was to go up and down three flights of stairs with a small child and a baby. She told him how happy she was to be able to see trees and grass growing and watch her children play outdoors.

Children playing along Ascension Street in Cherry Hill Village. Ascension Street is the only "street" in Cherry Hill Village

In February 1946, Mayor McKeldin dedicated Cherry Hill Homes at a program in the Community Center building attended by the residents and City officials. Dr. Murphy was on the program along with his replacement on the housing authority board, Furman L. Templeton. The Mayor praised the service of Dr. Murphy whose term he had extended so that Dr. Murphy could see the fruition of the 600-unit Cherry Hill project. Mr. Pinkett and Mrs. Burge were also on the program. Mr. Pinkett addressed the residents of Cherry Hill Homes saying, "This is a transfer point for you. Many of you are veterans from the war, and you should think in terms of only staying here [in public housing] temporarily. You should think in terms of buying a home and rearing a family." Mrs. Burge told the Mayor and other officials, "We, the residents, are so thankful to have new and decent homes with grass and open space for our children to play. We pledge to take care of our homes and our community. The lives we lead will be an expression of our gratitude and a testament to the faith you have put in us."

On July 11, 1951, Mayor Thomas D'Alesandro, Jr., father of Congresswoman Nancy Pelosi and Mayor Thomas D'Alesandro III, broke ground for Extension I of Cherry Hill Homes. Tyler, Ketcham, and Myers were awarded the contract as the Chief Architects, and they hired Hilyard R. Robinson, a noted black architect, as their associate architect. Robinson, a native Washingtonian, studied at the Philadelphia School of Industrial Arts prior to going into the Army in 1917 during WWI and serving in France. The story goes that Robinson was in Paris for the Armistice, and was so impressed with the architecture, he returned home in 1919 and transferred to the architecture program at the University of Pennsylvania. While working in Harlem as a draftsman during the summers of 1921 and 1922, he met Paul B. LaVelle, a practicing architect and Professor of Architecture at Columbia University. LaVelle assisted Robinson with a transfer to Columbia in 1922, and Robinson graduated with a B. A. in Architecture.

After receiving his M. A. from Columbia University in 1931, Robinson got married and toured Europe for 18 months as a Kinne Fellow, a traveling fellowship awarded to Columbia students to encourage them to expand their education through travel. He continued his studies in Berlin at the Ausland Institute, and he traveled around to France and Scandinavia photographing post-WWI construction techniques and government sponsored housing solutions.

Robinson returned to Washington to teach architecture at Howard University at its new School of Architecture where he served as instructor

Private homes along Booker T Drive in Dupont Manor

and Chair until 1937. While there, he designed 11 Howard buildings. He co-designed Langston Terrace Dwellings, the first black public housing project, in 1936, and he designed a number of residences for his fellow faculty at Howard University, including a house for Nobel Peace Prize laureate Ralph Bunche. This residence is located in the Brookland neighborhood of Washington, D. C. Robinson also received the first defense contract given to a black person to design and build the Tuskegee Army Air Field.

When Robinson left Howard, he sought to apply the European, low-cost housing construction techniques he had studied to benefit black Americans. He became Chief Architect for the Public Works Administration in 1935, and from 1950 to 1955, he served on the National Capital Planning Commission and was the Director of the Washington Housing Association. Extension 1, consisting of 637 more public housing units, opened in November 1952. This included houses on Carver, Bethune, Bunche Roads and Coppin Court. Also, in 1952, the HABC purchased Cherry Hill Homes back from the FPHA for $3,423,663.89.

Mayor D'Alesandro dedicated Extension II on November 1, 1956. This section had the unique distinction of being designed with convertible apartments that could be increased or decreased to meet the demands of various sized families. As many as 400 units could be created from the 360 units built; or they could be condensed to 300 apartments. Cherry

Public housing along Claflin Court

Hill was the first place in the country to use this concept to maximize the availability of housing as required by the sizes of tenant families on waiting lists.

The convertible apartment was the brain child of artist and architect Dano Jackley. Jackley was from Frankton, Indiana, where he attended the John Herron Art Institute from 1919 to 1922. From 1925 to 1926 he studied architecture at the Georgia Institute of Technology. Jackley moved to Baltimore and worked for the Chesapeake & Potomac Telephone Company, the forerunner to Verizon, as an architect from 1929-1948 before starting his private architectural practice. He then went on to join the architectural firm of Taylor and Fisher who received the contract to design Extension II.

The Housing Authority requested of the firm, "Can you give us apartments adjustable as to size?" Jackley's solution was doorways that could be opened or closed with wall-like closures within 15 or 20 minutes. These apartments could be increased from one to five bedrooms, with some capable of being converted into duplexes. With this flexibility, the problem arose of how to handle plumbing because no units could have more than one kitchen or bathroom. Under Jackley's plan, a former bathroom became a roomy closet, and a former kitchen became a dining room or bedroom.

The opening of Extension II in 1956 completed the original core of the Cherry Hill community. For the first time in the history of Baltimore City,

Rental apartments on Seagull Avenue The smoke stacks of the incinerator are directly behind Cherry Hill Village

a variety of brand new housing became available to its black residents. At this time, Cherry Hill housed approximately 10,000 residents with 30 percent of the households being homeowners and 70 percent being renters, but all being one community. The first black planned, suburban community in the United States was well on its way.

3.

Paradise Found!

Our lives went from black and white to Technicolor when we moved to Cherry Hill. It was a vast change from viewing life in the city. Everything in Cherry Hill was shiny and new. There were woods full of blooming flowers and a waterfront that, although polluted, let you see out into forever. Cherry Hill Village and Cherrywood had waterfront views. According to James Dow, "My parents, Elsie and Adam Dow, moved to Bridgeview Road in late 1944. They were renting, and I can remember that our front steps were unfinished cinder blocks. I also remember that Reedbird Avenue was wet land covered with cattail plants before being developed. It was like living in the country."

Linda Bowman's mother and father, Oscar and Edith Dilver Bowman, moved into an apartment in Cherry Hill Village as newlyweds in 1944. Linda said, "My mother told us that she and my father had a one-room apartment in the city. One day my father, who worked at Continental Can Company, gave my mother money to put down on a house in Cherry Hill. When my father came home, he asked for the details about the house. Instead of telling him, my mother took my father to Cherry Hill to show him a brand new, fully furnished second floor apartment she had rented at 3022 Seamon Avenue." According to Linda, "My mother said that a man offered her an apartment for $1.50 a week, and she could not refuse an offer like that. She thought it made more sense to take the apartment and spend the rest of the money to furnish the apartment."

Salima Louise Siler Marriott Gibbs remembers riding the train to Pumphrey, Maryland, at the age of four and seeing Cherry Hill being built.

"In Maryland, as it occurred in other slave-holding states, free African Americans and emancipated slaves established communities following the Civil War. One such community is Pumphrey, located in northern Anne Arundel County and not far from Cherry Hill. My first recollection of Cherry Hill was when I rode the train to Pumphrey with my Mom to visit former Sandtown/Harlem Park neighbors who had moved there. My Mom pointed out Cherry Hill to me and said she wanted us to move there when the construction was finished. In 1945, our family consisted of my mom and dad, Cordie and Jessie Siler, my 13-year-old brother Jesse, my two-year-old brother James, and myself. James and I were turning 3 and 5 respectively, and my mom was pregnant with my sister Gloria.

"It was not a sure thing that we would be accepted for housing in Cherry Hill because my dad was not a veteran. In January 1946, we were notified that our application had been accepted for Cherry Hill Homes, and we moved into our three-bedroom, two-story new home with front and back porches and lawns at 2909 Spellman Road just days before Gloria was born on January 31. It was a bittersweet time because my brother Jesse, who had been my head start teacher who prepared me for school and told me daily that I was very smart, did not move to Cherry Hill with us. He decided to stay with relatives with whom he had lived while we waited for suitable housing because there were no schools in Cherry Hill and public transportation was limited. So while Cherry Hill represented a new beginning, the most significant impact on the Siler family was that my brother Jesse never returned to live with us."

"My parents, brother, and I moved to 717 Roundview Road, a 3-bedroom end unit, in 1947 when I was six months old," said Romaine Green Rucks. "My father was a crane operator at Bethlehem Steel, and my mother occasionally worked outside the home when we were older. One of the things I remember most about the neighborhood was the woods out back. I remember sitting in my window watching rabbits and deer. My brother and I often played in the woods picking blackberries and apples. My only bad memory was the morning my dog, Rex, came crawling home filled with buckshot. He had been shot by a man we called Farmer Brown, a recluse who lived on the other side of the woods. My mother stayed up all night trying to help Rex, but he died from his wounds."

Gwendolyn Burns Lindsay's parents bought a house on Ascension Street in Cherry Hill Village. "When my parents moved to Cherry Hill, they already had my sister, Sieglinda, who was one at the time. I came along the next year followed by my brothers Roderick and Rudolph. We were under seven and shared the second bedroom which contained two twin beds—the girls slept in one and the boys slept in the other. When Edith, Howard, Anthony, Myrika, and Kim came along, the basement was converted from the entertainment center for my parents to a bedroom for the boys. Daddy and Mommie were very skilled with tools and the sewing machine, and they managed to give us a beautiful home."

John Nelson, Jr., was eight in 1944 when his father, John, Sr., moved him, his mother, Clara, his brother, James, and his sister, Betty, to Cherry Hill from Winston Salem, North Carolina. According to John, "My father moved to Baltimore in 1943 to work for the shipyards. I believe there was a policy that able-bodied men either had to go into the military or work in the defense industry. There was no defense industry in Winston Salem, so my father moved to Baltimore. He brought us up a year later, and we moved to 3034 Seamon Avenue. At that time, Cherry Hill was like living in the country. I sat on my front steps and watched them cut through the woods to build Potee Street. A city cemetery was up the hill, and it emitted a tremendous stench. However, we were together as a family in a brand new apartment. My brother and I made friends with the other children in the area, and I felt like it was paradise."

On the other side of the hill, in June 1946, Lillian and Calvin Thomas, Sr., purchased 2705 Booker T. Drive, one of the homes in Dupont Manor. Their sons, Calvin, Jr. and Walter, were both delivered at home in Cherry Hill. Calvin said, "My parents moved from West Baltimore to Cherry Hill because it was a chance to purchase a new home and to raise a family in an environment that was so different from the city. We loved living in Cherry Hill because it set us on the best course we could have had for successful lives. We had an opportunity to see our parents and the other adults shape our community."

The 600 initial public housing units filled quickly. Elizabeth (Betty) Pinkney Harris was almost four when her family moved to 2715 Spelman Road, Apartment 3-A, early in 1946. Betty said, "My father had just returned from the navy when my parents learned of this new community being developed for veterans returning from World War II. There were five of us then—my parents, Willard and Beulah Pinkney, my older brother, Joe (Joseph); my older sister Penny (Dolores), and me. In August, not long after our arrival in Cherry Hill, my younger sister, Pat (Patricia) was born. I can still remember how much we enjoyed our childhood. Cherry Hill was one big happy family. Everybody was your friend, and I can't remember fearing anything."

"The three of us were free to roam throughout the community, and some of our best times were spent exploring the construction of the "new" projects as we called them. We got to know the night watchman and would frequently spend time listening to stories he would tell us. We would venture through the "woods" picking blackberries, crab apples, and wild cherries. When we wanted crabs, we would go crabbing with my father down on Potee Street. By 1956, my parents had an opportunity to purchase their own home at 610 Cheraton Road behind the shopping center. By then, there were six of us children."

Janice Graham Solomon was born in Cherry Hill at 1006 Shellbanks Road, Apartment 2A. She is one of several babies delivered at home. "I was born in my parents' bedroom on May 14, 1947. Private homes were right across the street from us. We called them bungalows. The Van Hooks lived in the first house. They had no children and took a liking to me. They would give me a Christmas gift every year including a doll with a baby carriage, a table and chair set, and all sorts of girlie stuff. My brother, Louis, was friends with twins Freddie and Freda Greer who lived in another bungalow.

"Those of us from public housing and the children from the private homes all played together. They would come over where we lived and sit outside with our parents while we played on the grass in the evening before bath and bed. Every now and then, the Van Hooks would have my Mother and us over for lunch or in the evening. My Father always worked two jobs to support us, so he was rarely available for these events. My father passed away in 1953, and everyone was very supportive of us."

Veronica Thomas was also a home delivery. "My mother, Madeline Thomas, was already living in Cherry Hill at 2802 Round Road when I was born," said Veronica. "I was delivered at home by Dr. Jerry Luck, one of the three doctors practicing in Cherry Hill. I had two sisters who were much older than I was, and since my mother worked, I was sent to live with my grandparents, James and Ethel Butler, who lived a few blocks away at 1009 Slater Road so that they could raise me until I got old enough to take care of myself. I also had an aunt who lived in Cherry Hill. I was about ten before I moved back home with my mother."

In the spring of 1948, Sandra Green Johnson, moved to Cherry Hill when she was 6 months old. Her mother, Elsie, her sister Catherine, who was seven at the time, and her late brother Charles, six, moved into 2809 Spelman Road. Sandra said, "We were poor, but proud. We were raised to know who we were and what we could become, and for the most part, you saw that in your neighbors." Life for Sandra was good in Cherry Hill until her mother died when Sandra was 13. "I felt so alone, and our extended family seemed so far away in the city. I didn't know what would happen to me."

Charles had joined the Army when he turned 16. Catherine was in her second year in college. Fortunately for Sandra, the spirit of being good neighbors exemplified the early Cherry Hill community. Elsie Green and Madeline Thomas, Veronica's mother, not only were neighbors, they were also fellow parishioners at St. Veronica's Catholic Church. Mrs. Thomas shared her home with Sandra and Catherine until Catherine could graduate from college, get a better job, and she and Sandra could move to their own apartment.

My parents, John and Armenella Speaks Morris, moved to Cherry Hill because it was affordable. My father was a clerk for the Social Security Administration, and at one point, government employees were considered defense workers. There were several Federal employees who had been accepted only to find out that they did not qualify as defense workers. However they were allowed to stay until their incomes surpassed the maximum allowed for eligibility in public housing.

We moved to 2902 Carver Road in April 1953 in the first extension. We had a row house with eight houses to the row. At that time, there were trees across the street in front of us and a woods on the other side of the crossroad. We were on the corner of Bridgeview Road, and along Bridgeview Road there were several bungalow style houses that were there well before we came. I was a month shy of turning five-years-old.

Up until I was four, I lived in a large, 3-story row house at 517 N. Gilmor Street in the Harlem Park neighborhood of west Baltimore with my Mom, my sister Judy, an unmarried aunt, two married aunts and their husbands, and three cousins—11 people. My Mom, my older sister Judy and I shared a bedroom with Hilda, the unmarried aunt, on the second floor. My Aunt Dot, Uncle Charles, and my cousins, Paula and Nancy had bedrooms on the second floor. My Aunt Rose, Uncle James, and cousin, Leon, had their own apartment on the third floor. The first floor was a common area for all of us.

There was always someone cooking in the kitchen, and the kitchen was the place where we gathered. I loved that house! Even though it was a bit run down, it had to have been a grand house in its day. It had high ceilings with classic crown moulding, and a large living room with an ornamental fire place and mantel that we used as the backdrop for taking pictures. Although I wasn't born at the time, I'm told that my grandmother's casket was placed in front of the fireplace when she died on Christmas

Eve in 1945. Behind the living room was a grand staircase with a bannister that all the children in the house learned to slide down—except me because I wasn't old enough.

There were two things I wanted to get old enough to do, and they were to slide down the bannister and scrub the white marble steps on Saturdays with Ajax cleanser like my cousin Paula. She had to scrub those steps religiously every Saturday before she was allowed to do anything else. Then the rest of the week, the steps served as my perch for seeing the world. This included watching people passing by who would sometimes stop and speak. I watched cars and service trucks coming with their products or services, like the iceman or the coal man. If I was lucky, I could see an Arab (pronounced A-rab)—a man leading a horse-drawn wagon of fruits and produce—with his melancholy cry enunciating the names of all the items on his cart. The steps were about nine feet from the street, so I could not get off them without permission and someone to accompany me.

Just about the time I was turning four, my Mom married my Dad and we moved up town to a second floor, two bedroom apartment on Winchester Street, a nice area where blacks were beginning to buy houses. I tell you this because you need to understand that when we moved to Cherry Hill, I had never played outside on my own. My family now consisted of my Mom and Dad, Judy, and my two-week old brother, John. My Aunt Rose and Uncle James drove us to Cherry Hill and helped us move in at night. I was so excited that all I could do was run up and down the stairs.

From the time we lived on Gilmor Street, I was surrounded by books and magazines. My Aunt Rose had a whole wall of books that fascinated me. My mom and aunts used to read movie magazines and *Life*, *Look*, and all the homemaking magazines like *Ladies Home Journal*, and *McCall*. I had my own library of Golden Books—*Little Black Sambo* being my favorite. The night we moved to Cherry Hill, Aunt Rose gave me a new Golden Book, *Linda and Her Little Sister*, in an effort to improve my attitude towards my baby brother.

I remember taking my new book from Aunt Rose, and going to sit on Uncle James' lap for him to read it to me. As was customary for me when I got sleepy, I would suck the middle two fingers of my right hand, and when Uncle James started reading to me I was sucking my fingers. My mother said to me, "Stop sucking your fingers." No sooner was that said, when Uncle James said, "I'll fix this. Give me those fingers." As soon as I pulled them out of my mouth, he grabbed them and spit on them. Needless to say, I never put those fingers back in my mouth again. So while moving to

Cherry Hill was an overall joyous time, it was tinged with a little trauma for me.

The next morning my Mom let me play out in the back yard—a common lawn for all the houses in the row, with metal t-bar poles with hooks for putting up clothes lines to dry clothes for the eight houses in our row. After playing for a while, I wanted to go back in the house. I turned around to look at the row of back doors, but I could not remember out of which door I had come. They all looked alike. I chose one and knocked as hard as I could to get someone to let me in. Imagine my horror when a complete stranger answered the door. All I could do was cry, thinking that my family had abandoned me in favor of that baby! I was in a complete crying panic, the kind where you think you are talking but no one can understand you through the wails. Since we were the last ones to move into the block, the neighbor figured out where I came from and took me one door over to my house. I was so happy to see my Mom when she came to the door. She thanked the neighbor, Mrs. Aurelia Croslin, and let me back in. After calming me down, she laughed at me—just like the time I got the fish bone stuck in my throat, or the time I swallowed an ice cube. My mom could find humor in the worst situations. It took a while before I ventured out by myself again.

My sister, Judith (Judy) Campbell Graves, remembers that my Mom did not want to move to Cherry Hill. Judy said, "Mom told dad that she would move to Cherry Hill for five years, but after that, she wanted him to buy us a house. Mom missed her family, but they came to visit us because my uncles had cars and coming to Cherry Hill was like coming to the country—maybe a half-hour drive from our old west Baltimore neighborhood in those days. Also, because my Mom was a licensed hair dresser, my aunts came to get their hair done.

"Cherry Hill was a very friendly place. We had so much open space. You could walk around day and night, and no one would bother you. You felt really safe. People helped each other and looked out for one another. Cherry Hill was a fun place to be. Our cousins, Betty and Nancy, would come down and stay a week or two with us in the summer. They loved getting out of the city."

About the same time we were moving to Cherry Hill, so was the Pugh family. They moved to Cherry Hill in 1953 because it was an up-and-coming community for black families. At that time, there were the parents, Adolphus and Dorothy Pugh, and the first three children, Phillip, 5, Wesley, 3 and Candy, 2. They lived in a two-bedroom apartment in

Coppin Court, a new unit in the first extension. The Pughs had another child, Pam, in 1954, and became celebrities in June 1955 when Mrs. Pugh delivered the first set of triplets (they were actually quadruplets, but one child died in delivery) in Cherry Hill history. The Pugh triplets, Diane, David, and Debra, were featured in the *Afro* newspaper when they were born, and every year the *Afro* would do an update on them. At the time of their birth, Mr. Pugh had been laid off from his job at the printing company where he worked, and the *Afro* solicited help for the family. The Gerber company provided a year's supply of baby food, the Housing Authority relocated the family to a house on Bethune Road, and other local merchants stepped up to assist in the spirit of community that was indigenous to Cherry Hill. As if seven children weren't enough, the Pughs took in their niece, Kim, and raised her as one of their own. Cherry Hill embraced the Pugh family and facilitated the development of all the children throughout their formative years.

According to Wesley, "My mother assigned each of us older siblings a triplet to look after, an arrangement that continues to this day. Phil was assigned to look after Diane, the oldest triplet. I was assigned responsibility for Debra, the youngest triplet. My sister Candy was assigned to care for David, the middle triplet. For seven consecutive years, the Afro did a picture story on the Pugh triplets with a brief story and the ever-resistant pose by Debra, always nearly in tears; Diane, smiling for the camera; and David, just staring at the photographer." Each year, the Pugh triplets continued to thrive and the *Afro* continued to document their progress well into their young adulthood.

Rethia Roach Nickerson and her mom moved to 808 Bridgeview Road into the section built in Extension II. Rethia said, "We moved from a third floor tenement on Lexington Street in the city. I remember coming home from school, using the three keys that were on a string around my neck to first unlock the front door, climb three flights of stairs to the third floor; unlocking the door that led to that floor, then using the last key to unlock the door to our one room apartment. The kitchen was in one corner, the bedroom in another. There was no bathroom, except on the main hall, which we shared with the other occupants of the third floor. I think there were three apartments on our floor. I never used the bathroom unless my Mom was home. I entertained myself by looking out the window watching the traffic and people move below me.

"I don't know what the process was for getting an apartment in Cherry Hill. However, I remember how happy my mother was when she learned that we were accepted as tenants. I also remember how wonderful it felt to sleep there that first night with a bathroom of our own, a front door, back door, front porch, kitchen, refrigerator, a yard to play in and friends to play with. Our new home and community supplied all of our needs, except for a job for my working mother. She left daily to work with what must have been a new peace. Because of our neighbors, she could leave me knowing that I was safe and cared for while she worked.

"Thankfully I will never really know for sure, but I believe that moving to Cherry Hill Homes saved my life and my mother's life. She got her GED, went to nursing school and eventually became a college graduate and homeowner. The friends I made there remain the anchors of my village, my family!"

Frances Martin James' parents, Abraham and Mattie Martin, purchased a 3-bedroom end house on Seamon Avenue in 1955. Her father was also a veteran, having served with the Army in Italy, and was able to purchase their home on the GI Bill. "Dad worked for more than 30 years at Bethlehem Steel before retiring. When we moved to Cherry Hill, there were five of us children. My sisters Mamie, Gayle, Felecia, and I shared the largest bedroom, my brother Abraham had the smallest bedroom, and my parents took the middle bedroom."

The Martin family were living in Turner's Station, one of the public housing projects built earlier in Baltimore County, when they decided to purchase a home in Cherry Hill. Frances Martin James recollects, "My parents, Abraham and Mattie Martin Jr., moved me and my four siblings to 3015 Seamon Avenue in 1955. Dad worked the swing shift schedule for Bethlehem Steel, Sparrows Point, for many years in the wire division. Once everyone was in school, Mom worked as a domestic at $7 a day plus bus fare until she got a job, with benefits, as a paraprofessional in the public schools in Cherry Hill and nearby communities.

"We lived in an end house and Dad personally built the symbolic 'white picket' fence to frame our piece of the American dream. Later, a chain link fence was installed. We were next to a hill that used to be mostly trees. That mini-forest had fragrant honeysuckle vines, crab apple trees, berries, etc. and poke salad that we would pick and Mom would carefully prepare. Where else in the city could you do that?"

The Welch Family moved to 2829 Spelman Road in 1958 from 922 Bevan Street, a small alley in Sharp-Leadenhall, a South Baltimore neighborhood. According to Favia Welch Hicks, "I was nine-years-old and in fourth grade. My great-grandparents settled in South Baltimore with their 14 children in the early 1900's. The house we lived in had two bedrooms, a small kitchen and living room. There was one bathroom, a toilet room, that mom said had been installed right before we moved in. The bathroom had no sink or bath tub. Mom had to heat water for our use.

"We lived near dozens of cousins, aunts, grandparents and friends. My paternal grandmother and her family, two daughters and a son, lived a block away on Hamburg Street. My maternal grandmother, great-grandmother, and several cousins lived two blocks away in the 800 block of Leadenhall Street, and across the street from them lived another Aunt with her family. We were a poor, but tight-knit, clan.

"When two of Mom's closest cousins moved to Cherry Hill, we soon followed. Needless to say, the 3 bedroom home on Spelman Road with a full bathroom that had not only a sink, but also a tub, was luxury to us. The other intriguing part of the home for me was the small patch of grass that we called a "lawn" sitting in front of our home. We didn't quite know how to take care of it. My Dad didn't have a lawn mower so the grass grew extremely tall at first, and one of our nice neighbors finally cut it for us. All of the green space in the neighborhood, including the hills, gave me and my siblings a great place to run and play. It was like living in the country! It took getting used to the quiet. We weren't living so close to our family and friends anymore. Even Mom's two cousins and their families lived near the shopping center on the other end of Cherry Hill. I grew to love the solitude and serenity of Cherry Hill."

Charity Welch remembers, "When we lived on Bevan Street, my grandmother stopped by every day coming from work. We went around the block to visit my great-grandmother and many of our other cousins, aunts, uncles, etc., who also met at that house in the evenings. We were a close-knit family who enjoyed getting together. Moving to Cherry Hill meant not seeing our extended family as often.

On moving day, we shared a truck with my cousins who were also moving to Cherry Hill to live on Seabury Road. My mother said that while she was excited for the extra space and full bathroom, she was aware of the concerns of my extended family about the intrusion of the administrative control of the Housing Authority in the lives of families residing in public housing. As a five-year-old, I recall having mixed feelings of excitement for the new home, with a lawn and a tiny porch. My brother, Aaron, said he had never seen so much grass before. One of my early observations was that people in Cherry Hill did not scrub their steps in the evening—a ritual in the south Baltimore community. Like Favia, I, too, grew to love the solitude and serenity of Cherry Hill. We all did!"

4.

Learning to Play

Cherry Hill was a veritable toy chest full of play opportunities. The geography and landscaping of Cherry Hill afforded so many very creative play times. You didn't need play dates. You just moved in and went out and joined in whatever the kids on your block were doing. Summer meant being outdoors and getting tans and sunburns. I don't care what complexion we were when school was out in June because by September when school opened, we were all two shades darker. I think most neighborhoods in Cherry Hill were on the same schedule—especially since there was no air conditioning. Thank God for screen doors! Usually we would go out in the mornings before the hottest part of the day, come in for lunch, a nap, a bath, dinner, and go back outside for the evening in a fresh change of clothes.

There were games that were common to all the neighborhoods, and then there were activities that developed as a result of being in proximity to special features or natural resources like the woods, ponds, train tracks, etc. Those red clay cliffs mentioned earlier drew children to them, and in June 1949, two young residents seven and three were killed in a land slide of sand and clay from the cliffs. Many of our activities would be deemed unsafe today, and probably parents would have been charged with negligence or endangering minors. However, we didn't know any better back then because we were innocent and fearless and explored every inch of Cherry Hill to the fullest.

Judy remembers, "We had crab apple trees in our back yard and like clockwork, in the early spring caterpillars would hatch from the cocoons before the crab apples fully developed and started dropping. We had crab apple fights with our neighbors, the Braceys, a family with five children who lived on the other side of us in the end house. After the fights, we would go and do something else together. We played wagon train together with them and the other children on the block. There may have been four Red Flyer wagons among 12 children. Each wagon could hold three or four children—depending on how old and how big they were. The first two people in the wagon faced forward and the last person was the coupler and shock absorber. He or she sat backwards facing the wagon behind. This person had to hold the wagon handle of the wagon behind and place their feet on the wagon to keep it from bumping into the wagon in front of it. We would load the wagons at the top of the hill that our back yard came out to, and the front wagon would push off down the hill. What a ride! Then we'd drag the wagons back up the hill and do it all over again.

"If enough of us were outside, we played step ball or dodge ball, one-two-three red light, or mother-may-I. If no one else was out, we'd entertain ourselves with jump rope, jacks, pick-up sticks, or marbles. Dad played tennis, so we always had plenty of old tennis balls to use for our step ball games. He also bought us a badminton set which he set up in the back yard and taught us to play. When our mothers didn't have the clothes-lines up on the T-bar poles, we would climb them and swing from them. We didn't know it, but we were performing gymnastic routines.

"Sometimes we would ask for a clean mayonnaise or jelly jar so that we could put holes in the top and go hunt for bees, grasshoppers, praying mantises, as insects were prolific in Cherry Hill. In the evenings, we would try to catch lightning bugs in our jars and make what we called lamps, multiple lightening bugs blinking off and on intermittently. We would try to take off the lightning bug's light and make diamond rings—placing the light where a ring would go on our fingers, each time hoping that the light would stay on once detached from the bug. It never did.

"Usually on summer evenings, we sat on our porches. One of us might get out a View Master, and we would take turns looking at the different reels. The View Master showed things in 3D, and we had just about all of the fairy tales and well as travel reels showing the National Parks and other tourist sites in the United States. The View Master was like virtual reality goggles are today."

Janice loved to play hopscotch. She said, "While our mothers hung clothes in the courtyard, we would bring our little table and chair sets out with our dish sets and have tea parties using water or Kool-Aid. We would set up lemonade stands, and my friend, Carolyn Smith, had a coke machine, and we used to sell little cups of that.

Roderick remembers playing along the water front. "We had a Tarzan swing in the woods overlooking Waterview Avenue facing the Hanover Street Bridge and Middle Branch. It was large hemp rope (similar to the rope in the gym, but old and frayed) tied to a tree with a knot at the bottom. You would swing out holding on to the rope, and it seemed like you were swinging out into oblivion because there was a slight ravine beyond the tree. If you let go, you would roll down the cliff. We would go to the Tarzan swing after seeing the Saturday double feature at the Hill Theater. The woods were our jungle, and we explored and made trails. We played for hours often coming home with poison ivy, scratches, and ticks.

"The Harborview Townhouses were under construction, and many days the construction site was better than the playground or the football field. To be caught playing in them meant certain punishment. My parents did not approve of us playing outside the neighborhood. The area we lived in was often referred to as 'farmer land' perhaps because there were chicken coops, vegetable gardens and pigeon coops. I used to wring chicken necks and pick feathers, and we'd have them for dinner. I remember working for the neighbor cleaning her chicken coops, picking eggs in the morning, and weeding her garden to earn a quarter for spending.

"In back of our home was an open field and beyond it was a wooded area with lots of trees. On the other side of the trees was a small farm which belonged to a white man we called farmer Brown. His property had pear trees, peach trees, and apple trees which we scaled regularly for the fruit and were promptly run off by shots from his rifle. For some of us, this was our idea of fun never knowing the danger we were in.

"The field was used as a crude baseball field where we played ball with kids from all over Cherry Hill. Some evenings it was a major event because the teams may one day consist of all players from upper streets against players from the lower streets; and the games would last until dark.

"We made go-carts from fruit boxes used for shipping to the area markets and dumped on the city dump next to the incinerator. We would turn them into toys for fun using old skates, nails drawn from old wooden boxes, 2 x 4's from wood found and brought home from the dump. We also made wagons from baby carriage wheels, axles and parts that we scavenged from the dump."

Norma Jean Jackson Fortune also remembers trespassing on Farmer Brown's field. She said, "I was a real tom boy. My brother, his friends and I would come all the way from Windwood Court to pick fruit from his trees. Since I was the smallest one, they would boost me over the fence to get the fruit so that my brother could make pies for the whole neighborhood. One day I got over the fence and Farmer Brown's dogs came running at me. I started running toward the fence, but I couldn't make it. My brother told me to climb up the tree and stay up there until they came back to get me. They came back for me, and the next day we had pies!"

Play was usually gender specific, but there were times that there was crossover. I don't remember hearing that you can't do this because you are a girl, but the girls and boys just gravitated to different activities. "We made bottle dolls out of empty soda bottles and used rope twine as the hair. We would wet the twine, roll it up on brown paper, and let the twine dry. Voila! We had a nicely curled hair do for our bottle dolls," said Gwen, Roderick's sister. We also played with bat 'n balls, wooden paddles with a thin elastic rubber string, and when the string would break we would use toothpicks to stick the string back into the ball to last a make it last a little longer.

"We used empty car tires and rolled them down the back alley of Ascension Street to see whose tire would get to the bottom of the hill first. We also would place ourselves inside the tires and roll down the alley for joy rides. I followed the boys in doing this one time and got hurt. We would entertain ourselves for hours with the old Montgomery Ward or Spiegel Catalogs by cutting out the people in the front of the book and putting a slit in the beds in the back of the book and placing the people in the beds to go to sleep. We made our own paper dolls by cutting out the people in the catalogs and cutting the clothes displayed in other sections of the catalogs. We pasted the clothes on the dolls sometimes using paste made from flour and water."

Yvette recalls, "My brothers made skate boxes and scooters with the wooden boxes that fruits and vegetables stacked behind the A&P. They also used wooden soda crates. They were highly prized because of their weight, and the thickness of the wood. These were also stacked up behind the A&P or the drug store. We weren't supposed to take those, since the soda delivery trucks retrieved them every morning when they brought more sodas. However, anything left behind the stores, the kids felt was fair game!"

There was nothing like winter in Cherry Hill. The woods and the hills were very scenic when it snowed, and they presented quite a challenge. Most of us would get some type of outdoor toy like skates, bikes, wagons, sleds, etc., for Christmas. Houston Murphy remembers the times he spent with his playmates, "In the winter, me and my gang sledded down the hill behind Denham Circle. We played in the woods and shot rats in the dump. We played along the railroad tracks, followed the tracks to Pumphrey, and got into fights with the white kids from Brooklyn on our way to Pumphrey. They would call us niggers and throw stones at us, and we raided their yards and stole their apples and bikes. We sometimes hopped trains, and we put pennies on the railroad tracks and collected the smashed copper pennies. We got the train engineers to give us flares so that we could take them apart and play with fire.

"My gang, Steven Gary Lewis, Michael Holland, Michael Manigo, Arthur Ashe Knight, and I were influenced by westerns and World War II movies. I had a dirt hole in our back yard where the gang and I would play with plastic soldiers or cowboys and Indians and dig miniature caves, build mountains, create rivers, and make teepees out of twigs and newspaper. We'd play for hours. We created sound effects for whinnying horses, rifle shots, men dying, explosions, and whatever else we could imagine. We were in our own little world. We got so dirty. Not to mention, my cat, Ross, would occasionally use my dirt hole as his litter box. I can remember being stripped to my drawers and hosed off outside before I was allowed into the house."

Frances and her friends liked to play school. "Our play time was mostly with our Seamon Avenue and LaRue Square friends in the alley behind the two streets. We played the traditional street games, but we also played school with the worksheets our teachers would give us if they had extra copies. Although we lived on the private homes side of Seamon Avenue with the public housing across the street, there was no distinction between us. Most of the homeowners, like my parents, were first timers who formerly resided in public housing. There was no reason to feel any better than anybody else."

Alonzo Bailey remembers that Cherry Hill cultivated his love of nature, "I remember going fishing and crabbing at the yacht club off of Waterview Road. We used to hike the woods behind 180 where the red clay cliffs were. We called the woods clay mountain. We would go to the woods across from the shopping center to find frog eggs that we kept until they developed into tadpoles. Living in Cherry Hill gave us a great respect for nature."

Wes and his friends also loved growing up in what could have been a nature preserve. "Us guys would take hikes into the woods—usually seven to nine of us forming a single line—the oldest in front leading the way. Sometimes we would pick apples or blackberries, catnip, 'green tree cigars,' that we let ripen brown, or acorns. There were hollow plant stems that we made into pipes, to sneak off and smoke tobacco or just light up the tree cigars.

"The landscape in Cherry Hill was the perfect place to run and just leap in the air or off the edge of a cliff where we would land in a pile of sand that covered the beautiful red clay terrain. One of my most vivid memories was when three or four of us went into the woods without the older guys. We came across a stream of flowing water, which was not unusual to find, but on this occasion the water flowing through the wooded areas revealed a jet stream of water pushing up from the ground. We tasted and drank the water. In all my sixty plus years of life, to this day, I still have never tasted water as cold and refreshing as I did on that day in the woods in Cherry Hill."

One of the most seductive play areas was the train tracks that encircled the back side of the projects. The tracks were a natural lure for the boys. Wes and his friends used to flatten pennies on the track so that they could use them in vending machines as dimes. They would also wait for trains so that they could wave at the engineer, and as the train passed, jump up and down to get the attention of the conductor in the caboose to implore him to throw them flares. Says Wes, "And on cue, the conductor would appear with a handful of red flares which were used by train personnel to be lit and left on the track burning to let another train coming behind them know that there was a train up ahead. We never bothered the lit flares. We just ran and fought among ourselves to retrieve the flares that the conductor threw to us from the train. There was excitement in lighting your own flare, especially around the 4th of July when it seemed like the conductor threw us more. Usually, those of us lucky enough to come away with two or three flares ungrudgingly gave one to whoever didn't have one."

There was nothing like going for a swim on a hot summer day. Wes said, "I can remember going to the swimming pool on a regular basis in the summer. The lifeguards would let me and my guys climb over the pool fence and pay them half the cost of admission, and we could swim all day! Afterwards, on our way home, we took the money we saved and went to this old man who made snowballs—the Baltimore way. He shaved his ice really fine into the card board snow ball tray, and then he sprinkled—not poured—on the flavoring. Then he added the wooden snowball spoon. What a refreshing way to end the day."

We learned so much from our play. It taught us the value of team work, and that everybody has a contribution to make. We learned how to improvise because while we could not always afford the real thing, we could create something that approximated the experience. Most of all, we learned to value our thoughts and ideas and the journey to bring them to life. Cherry Hill was a bodacious playmate.

5.

And he Rested on the Seventh Day

After turning right onto Cherry Hill Road from Waterview Avenue and driving about a mile, you come to what is called "church corner." It is here you will find five of the six denominations to establish churches in Cherry Hill by 1955. St. Veronica's Catholic Church and Christ Temple Apostolic Church are on the left, and First Baptist Church of Cherry Hill, Cherry Hill Presbyterian Church, and Hemingway Temple African Methodist Episcopal (A.M.E.) Church occupy a square on the right. The first denomination to have a presence was the United Methodist Church which began organizing in 1944.

Methodism in Cherry Hill started out in a home borrowed by Reverend Arthur White, a minister from another newly developed Baltimore public housing project, Turner's Station. The home was located on Joseph Avenue in the center of the private home developments. Reverend White went door-to-door in the developments telling the residents of his mission and asking for their help. When Reverend White's congregation began to outgrow the house, they went to the Washington Methodist Conference and asked for assistance. The Conference gave Reverend White a check for $1,000 to use as a down payment for the property located at the corner of Bridgeview and Round Roads, that had a house and an abandoned machine shop situated on it.

Reverend White moved his family into the house and held services there until the men of the congregation could get the machinery moved out of the shop. Once the shop was vacant, the congregation cleaned it up and started using it for services. The congregation, lead at that time by Reverend Nathaniel P. Perry, marched into its current edifice in May 1960.

I remember worshipping in the old church, the one level, cinder block, flat-roof building which had been the machine shop. Although our family tradition was deeply rooted in African Methodism, founded by Richard Allen as an offspring of the Methodist Church, my mother took us to services at Cherry Hill Methodist church because it was right behind our house on Carver Road. When we attended, Reverend Alfred Vaughn was the minister. I remember him always being in a suit and wearing a hat looking somewhat like Dr. Martin Luther King. He made regular visits to the homes of his members and encouraged them to take parts in the organizations of the church. My mother had taken voice lessons and had a beautiful singing voice. Reverend Vaughn tried to encourage her to sing on the choir. Perhaps because my mother knew that she did not plan to stay in Cherry Hill, she never joined the choir.

Reverend Michael Braxton, father of TV's Braxton Family, grew up in Cherry Hill and attended the Methodist Church. He says, "Before the NFL ruled Sundays, the churches in Cherry Hill reigned supreme. Church attendance was fortified by the Blue Laws that forbade retail stores to be open on the Lord's day. The church was a place where the community rallied together in worship and praised God for the hard work that was done during the week. There was no option in the Braxton home on Swale Avenue on Sunday morning when Mr. McClarin came down the street and blew the car horn for the children in the neighborhood to go to Sunday School.

"As I grew older, I came to understand that the objectives of the church were to win people to Christ, preserve our culture, never let us forget how far we had come, and to encourage us—no matter how strong the opposition was—we should continue to press forward for a better life. I loved going to church because I met lifelong friends and adults who helped shape the neighborhood. Mostly, I remember that pretty little girl with lovely hair who used to sit next to me in Sunday school."

Although it was not the first religion with a presence in Cherry Hill, St. Veronica's Catholic Church had, by far, the biggest footprint. Carrying on a long tradition of service to Baltimore's black Catholic population, the Josephites launched a venture to service the young families flocking to the new community. In 1945, Fr. John Albert, S.S.J., pastor of St. Francis Xavier Church in East Baltimore, made a visit to Cherry Hill and saw the potential for the Church. He found 30 Catholic families there, and in July

1946 he requested permission from the Archdiocese to purchase 11 lots along what was then Cherry Hill Avenue for $9,000.

At that time, most of the black Catholics in South Baltimore attended St. Monica's Catholic Church. St. Monica was established as a parish in 1918 with Fr. John Dorsey, S.S.J., a black Josephite, as Pastor. Originally, the church was located at Henrietta and Hanover Streets, but in 1923, it relocated to a more prominent site on Henrietta and Eutaw Streets. That site housed the church, the rectory, a combination hall and school which was staffed by the Oblate Sisters, a black order of Nuns. St. Monica's closed in 1959 when the area became increasingly industrial. The St. Monica church complex was located on the site that currently houses Baltimore's Horseshoe Casino which is about 10 minutes from Cherry Hill.

Favia told me, "We were members of St. Monica's before moving to Cherry Hill. We used to walk over the Hamburg Street Bridge to church on Sunday. It was an all-black parish, but the priest was white. I remember making my First Communion when I was 7 years old."

Ida Welch, the Welch family matriarch, remembers, "My cousins and I attended St. Monica's School. The Nuns were very kind to us and wanted us to be smart. We loved being together as family while going to school, and we loved school. Education has always been a Welch family value. We knew it would make life better."

Fr. Francis Robbins, S.S.J., was the first priest assigned to the new mission parish in Cherry Hill in September 1946. He was born in Mexico City in 1910, and attended St. John's Preparatory School in Danvers, Massachusetts, before entering St. Charles College and Seminary which is now the site of the Charles Town Retirement Community in Catonsville, Baltimore County. Fr. Robbins was ordained in 1943 and was appointed the assistant Pastor at St. Monica's. He was living at St. Monica's when he was appointed as the pastor of St. Veronica's in 1946. Since there was no church or rectory, he continued to live at St. Monica's and travel back and forth daily to Cherry Hill visiting the sick, making house to house visitations, instructing children and adults in the Catholic faith, and planning for the future church. He said Mass every Sunday either at the Community Center, the Hill Theater, or another location in the Shopping Center as the parish grew.

"My mother, Madeline Thomas, was a founding member of St. Veronica's," said Veronica. "St. Veronica was a major part of my life. I was the first baby born in the parish, and my mother let Fr. Robbins name me. Fr. Robbins named me after St. Veronica. I grew up being told that I had wiped the face of Jesus—the 6th station of the cross. As a child, I kept trying to figure out when I had met Jesus. I loved being named after our church. I loved saying my name is Veronica, and I go to St. Veronica's on Veronica Avenue. No one else had that distinction."

By 1951, Archbishop Francis P. Keough approved the purchase of additional lots on what was by then Cherry Hill Road for $14,000, half of which was paid by the Archdiocese and half by the Josephites. This property had a tavern on it, a one-story frame building which Fr. Robbins and his parishioners converted to a rectory, with the bar area converted to a small chapel where Fr. Robbins said daily Mass. Fr. Robbins had sleeping quarters behind the chapel and a parlor area in the basement.

"The Colored Harvest" is a monthly newsletter that chronicled the progress of the church. The May 1951 edition tells of how students from St. Mary's Seminary at Roland Park in Baltimore, a Sulpician Seminary, were assigned to work with Fr. Robbins to harvest the families of Cherry Hill and bring them to Catholicism. Robert E. Hiltz, one of the Seminarians, describes the journey as follows, "Permission was given to inaugurate this unusual walk in October 1949. It was unusual because Cherry Hill is unusual. Cherry Hill is the name of a vast, modern housing development for Negroes off the Annapolis Highway [Old Annapolis Road] just over the Hanover Street Bridge. It is sandwiched between Westport and Brooklyn in the city of Baltimore.... At present, there are more than 12,000 persons living in Cherry Hill. Soon, when the new houses are opened, there will be close to 20,000. Almost 5,000 of these are children, and we see only a few of them .... Away from debilitating character-corrupting slums, these children, for the first time in their lives, are enjoying green grass, trees, playgrounds, wide streets, freedom from traffic and uncramped, uncluttered houses. Cherry Hill has its own shopping center, with stores of all kinds, plus a movie. One church is being built, and both the Catholics and Presbyterians own land for churches to come. There are no taverns in all of Cherry Hill."

The seminarians were welcomed into Cherry Hill by R. Clarke Davis, the second manager of Cherry Hill Homes, and his staff as they performed their functions. Mr. Davis was located in the Community Center building as were all of the City agencies represented in Cherry Hill which at that time, among them the Department of Recreation, the Public Welfare Department, and the Enoch Pratt Library. The seminarians organized summer athletic and Vacation Bible school programs for the children as a way of networking with the families. Hiltz documented how by playing dodge ball and football with a group of about 30 initial children, and holding catechism classes led to over 300 children showing up for their first Christmas Party.

Fr. Robbins went door-to-door taking a census of the families in Cherry Hill while seeking to attract families to Catholicism. One of the activities he instituted was an annual summer carnival. The men of the church built booths and the women would make food for sale at the booths. They made codfish cakes, crab cakes, hot dogs, potato salad, and all sorts of cakes and pies. There was a ferris wheel and other rides for the children. All of the community would come out to support the carnival, and the church would gain new members.

By late 1953, Fr. Robbins membership grew from 325 in 1946 to 593, and he began planning to build the much-needed church. However, on the night of New Year's Day 1954, Fr. Robbins died in a fire in the rectory. According to accounts by the Fire Department, the fire started in the parlor below his bedroom and was attributed to faulty wiring. While the fire did not burn the upstairs rooms, Fr. Robbins and his dog died from the smoke that came up through the open louver in the bedroom floor. He was transported to South Baltimore General Hospital where he was pronounced dead on arrival. Fr. Charles T. Coughlin, S.S.J., was named to succeed Fr. Robbins on January 31, 1954, and he built the church which stands today and was dedicated on May 1, 1955, by Archbishop Keough.

The Presbytery of Baltimore began organizing in Cherry Hill in July 1947 with 100 applicants for membership. Reverend Casper I. Glenn was ordained in the spring and sent along with E. Valeria Murphy to start Sunday School classes which they conducted in the Community Center auditorium. In July 1952, Reverend Edgar W. Ward was appointed to succeed Reverend Glenn, and it was under his leadership that a one-story building was erected that later became the basement of the church that was dedicated on June 2, 1963, by Reverend E. Rudolph Obey.

"Our family attended Cherry Hill Presbyterian Church during the ministries of Reverends Ward and Obey. It was truly at church that was involved with the community with daily activities under the watchful, stern and loving guidance of E. Valeria Murphy, Director of Christian Education," said Madeline Murphy Rabb (no relation), a member of one of Baltimore's most prominent families and one of Cherry Hill's founding families. "Her quiet demeanor belied a brilliant, caring teacher and mentor to many children and adults in Cherry Hill, including my mother, Madeline Wheeler Murphy.

"I have warm memories of spending lots of time in the church with friends and family in Sunday school, Brownies, choir, etc. My father, William, was an elder. My mother, who had a beautiful soprano voice, was a member of the choir and a soloist. One of my fondest memories was when my mother was in the annual Christmas pageant and played Mary. I also remember sitting nervously and anxiously in the congregation when my mother sang solos during the Easter service.

"My mother initiated and managed the annual rummage sales along with Elise Locksly. My mother taught Sunday school and later became Director of Christian Education when E. Valeria Murphy left to take that position at 6th Presbyterian Church in Chicago. My parents' participation in the church ended when the church leadership would not allow the Black Panthers to initiate a free breakfast program at the church."

Gwen adds, "I remember the confirmation classes and my mother making those white Confirmation dresses. Confirmation classes inserted white flowers on the cross on the altar after singing, "Oh Jesus I Have Promised. All eight of my siblings were entrenched in the activities of the church while growing up. My mother served faithfully in many capacities until she died."

In May 1948, the First Baptist Church started out in the 2500 block of Round Road with Reverend John II. Clark as its pastor, 25 members and a treasury of $30.50. When the membership increased to 75 by the end of the year, the church moved to a building on Woodview and Carver Roads. It wasn't until the spring of 1950 that the church moved to its current location on Cherry Hill Road.

Reverend William E. Clapp is credited with bringing African Methodism to Cherry Hill in the spring of 1950. He was an aging minister who laid the foundation for Reverend Melvin Chester Swann, a newly ordained minister, who was dispatched to continue the work begun by Reverend Clapp. The Baltimore Conference, a part of the 2nd Episcopal District which was administered by Bishop Lawrence Henry Hemingway, gave $2,000 to purchase a lot at Woodview Road and Booker T Drive for the establishment of Hemingway Chapel A.M.E. However, Mrs. Edith Holland Bryant, the wife of Reverend Harrison J. Bryant (who was elevated to Bishop in 1964) the pastor of Bethel A.M.E. Church in Baltimore, suggested that the name be changed to Hemingway Temple.

Reverend Swann held his first service in the Hill Theater with just a few persons present. As the summer months approached, the church was moved outdoors under a tent. They built a pulpit and purchased a piano and chairs for the tent to hold services for the months of July and August. However, on July 21, 1950, a fire destroyed the tent and its contents, and the church went back temporarily to worship in the Hill Theater. Then, Harry Myerburg, owner of the shopping center, offered the small congregation a vacant store in which to worship. On August 13, there was a ground-breaking ceremony with political dignitaries from the State and City, with Bishop Hemingway delivering the address. The Druid Construction Company was awarded the contract to build the church, and on Sunday, April 15, 1951, the congregation marched the four-blocks from the shopping center to the new edifice.

Margaret C. DuBois Smith was going on 16 when she walked with the 50 or so other members into the new sanctuary. "It was a beautiful, sunny day, and I walked along with my late brother James, who was 10, and my late sister Louise who was 14. We walked with Mrs. Mildred Jones who was the Sunday School Superintendent. The spirit of the crowd was high and very thankful that this had been accomplished. We marched into the church and left the doors open throughout the service so that people could come in and join us or just look in from the outside. We sat on folding chairs until the 1960s at which time we were able to purchase pews. We just celebrated our 65th anniversary."

The last church to locate at church corner was the Christ Temple Apostolic Church, organized by Elder Clenso Robinson, 29. He started the church in the building vacated by the Baptist church at Carver and Woodview Roads in 1951, and the congregation worshipped there until 1954 when they had to vacate the property because the City was building Extension II for Cherry Hill Homes. On March 11, 1954, Reverend Robinson died and was replaced by Elder Willard E. Saunders (who rose to become Bishop and head of the District of Columbia, Delaware, and Maryland Council of the Pentacostal of the World by the time he died in 1994). Elder Saunders purchased the lot at 827 Cherry Hill Road, and he and some of the men of the church built the structure themselves. The congregation marched into their new structure on December 25, 1954.

We were all defined by two institutions—what schools and churches we attended. It was just a given that families were affiliated with a Church. In the spring when we saw the line of girls in their white dresses with their veils processing through the streets close to St. Veronica's, every girl wanted to be Catholic. Gwen says that she remembers her mother making many of the white dresses being worn by the girls for their First Communion. "Our house would have dress parts strewn over door knobs, hanging from doors, and the like."

Veronica remembers her First Communion, "I was so excited to turn 7 so I could participate in receiving Communion on Sunday. Girls wore white dresses and white veils. Boys wore white suits. There was a ceremony in church and a procession outside after Mass. At the end of all of the morning festivities, breakfast was served in the church hall."

Janice said, "My mother would get up at 4 a.m. on Sunday to make rolls and set them aside to rise and then go to mass up the street at the Community Center. She would come back home and start breakfast while we got ready to go to Sunday school at the Presbyterian Church. We had our choice of corn flakes, cream of wheat or waffles with kidney stew. I was always dressed first and put out side with one of my dolls to wait for my siblings to get dressed. One of our neighbors, Betty White, would watch me while I was out there. Often people would pass by and say to me, 'My you look nice,' and give me money to put in my purse. One Sunday, a derelict man came by looking for handouts. I didn't know any better, so I said to him, 'My you look nice.' He then turned around and gave me money.

"Every Sunday my mother fried three chickens so we would have something to munch on until dinner was ready. Dinner would be a roast, a ham or something else good and always a prepared dessert. Anyone could stop by and get something good to eat until after the kitchen was cleaned up, and then she would say this is not a restaurant. We had to be home to sit down for dinner together and say grace. Our mother never sat down. She just stood over us and made sure everyone was served and nothing ran out. We realized later that she ate small portions while tasting so that she could serve us and any guests we had at our table."

Rethia reflects, "Having all the churches on one corner was a beautiful thing. We would walk together to church and then meet again afterwards to walk back home. With no air conditioning in the summer, of course the windows were up, and when the singing and sermons got lively, you could hear them all over. You could say that on Sunday afternoons, Cherry Hill made a joyful noise unto the Lord from church corner."

6.

Reading, Writing, and Arithmetic

The story of segregated schools in Cherry Hill is one of triumph, dedication, excellence and commitment that unfolded against a backdrop of separation steeped in legal, political and racial tension. Segregated schools in general were forced to operate within a culture of low expectations, discrimination, and negative views bestowed upon them because of laws and policies sanctioned by those holding the power. Negative views and labels aimed at segregated schools provided the catalyst to deem black students as less than, inferior and incompetent. Despite the beliefs and actions of many naysayers, scores of students from Cherry Hill rose high above those negative views and made impressive contributions to the society at large. In fact, their stellar accomplishments have been the driving force to substantiate the lack of merit and substance in traditional discourse. How was it possible, based on pervasive beliefs, that students could be so successful in schools that were very separate and indeed unequal? The history of schools in Cherry Hill revealed several intertwined factors including, well prepared and caring teachers, the value families placed on education, community schools and concern from the larger community that operated simultaneously to produce their impressive student outcomes in segregated schools.

It has been frequently documented that segregated schools used second hand textbooks sent from higher resourced white schools. That was true in Cherry Hill as well. However, the teachers in Cherry Hill and many other segregated communities across the country took steps to counter those shortages and any other perceived obstacles placed before them.

These schools in Cherry Hill employed stellar teachers, prepared at Coppin State Normal School, now Coppin State University, who possessed a profound sense of pride in accomplishment for themselves as well as the students they taught. With support from families and communities, they debunked the pervasive belief that black students were not competitive with white students and that black students' education only prepared them for low wage and service jobs.

To the contrary, the Breihan history contained an analysis of the planning and development of Cherry Hill using residents' oral histories and described the community as a powerhouse for producing talented black leaders "across the community, state, nation and the world." In his study, he further sought to gain an understanding of what it was like to attend school in Cherry Hill. One respondent offered the following, "It was great. It was a lot of feelings like family, friendship and unity. The teachers were from the old school; they were very dedicated to the job, it was almost like you were at home. But the teacher was almost like your family, your mom and your dad."

John Nelson explains how residents educated their children before schools were built in Cherry Hill. "When we moved to Cherry Hill in 1944, there were no schools. Parents could send their children to school wherever they chose. My parents sent me to Fairfield Elementary School because it was in the general area going towards Glen Burnie where my parents conducted a lot of their business. My brother, James, and I and two children down the street went to Fairfield. The children at Fairfield beat us up every day because they thought that we acted as though we were better than they were. I transferred to Cherry Hill Elementary School #159 when it opened in September 1946. I was in the fifth grade. We had a large playground surrounded by woods. One of my favorite memories is going to the woods in the fifth and sixth grades with our teacher, Mr. George Irvin Bryan, to chop down Christmas trees for our classroom. While we were in the woods, we picked up acorns, pine cones, and anything else we could use as decorations. When we got back to our classroom, we painted the pine cones and made other ornaments and paper chains. Those were special Christmases."

So while resources were often scant, using resource access as an indicator of education quality distorts the picture and minimizes the hard work invested in nurturing students and their talents. Thus, this perception of inequality, while not totally inaccurate, is however, one-sided.

Needless to say, Cherry Hill schools were built during an era when African American children saw few African American leaders outside of their own communities, but children revered school principals, teachers, ministers, and other community leaders. Black characters depicted on television and in the movies were usually shown as maids, chauffeurs, and other servants who often spoke incorrect English with the purpose of making others laugh. For many outside of the black community, those images formed their reality about black people.

Favorite television shows for children, who were fortunate enough to have a television set, were the Mickey Mouse Club, Mighty Mouse and the Romper Room with Ms. Nancy, originated in Baltimore in 1953, who had a magic mirror that allowed her to see which children were watching from home. Ms. Nancy was actually an early version of learning through media where children learned pre-reading skills watching the Romper Room Show. Life was much simpler for children who often believed that Ms. Nancy could really use her magic mirror to see them playing along at home.

At the core of the education story in Cherry Hill is the adults—the teachers, principals, custodians, secretaries, crossing guards, substitute teachers, etc. who all played a pivotal role in the education and social-emotional development of students in the community. Adults nurtured and watched over children and in return, children had great respect for the adults in the community.

Teachers held a very high status in the community and were highly respected and trusted by parents to make the right decisions with children entrusted to their care. There was a strong bond and mutual trust between parents and teachers. As a matter of fact, educators were often given parents' permission to discipline children who misbehaved in school. The teachers' word was sacrosanct.

Cherry Hill Elementary School # 159 was the first school built in Baltimore City in eight years. It was built to accommodate 680 children and opened with 815 that required the school to put 4 classes on part-time. Located at Cherryland and Bridgeview Roads, it opened with Mrs. Enna Payne as the Principal. In a March 1947 article in the *Baltimore Bulleting of Education: A Journal of the Public Schools of Baltimore, Maryland,* Mrs. Payne extoled the state of the art features of the building: large classrooms with running water; a public address system in each classroom; a heating and ventilation system that changed the air flow in the room without opening the windows; fire alarms; tiled walls from floor to ceiling; convertible bulletin boards that pivoted to reveal coat closets; and a kindergarten room with a fireplace.

Mrs. Payne was asked what caused the overcrowding of the school, and she responded, "When the Cherry Hill housing project was begun, it was simply a Government project; but since then three other privately owned developments have been set up. More people have moved to Cherry Hill than anyone expected." Mrs. Payne took the visiting journalist to the first classroom and said, "I want you to notice how nicely the children are dressed—how neat and clean they are—even though many of them come from really poor families."

When the journalist remarked on the "shiny cleanliness" of everything, Mrs. Payne explained how the staff trained the children to have "consideration for the rights and property of others." This caused the children to take care of not only the school, but other parts of the community as well. She said, "For instance, they do not walk on the lawn in front of the school, and they don't want anyone else to walk on it either. They are living in an entirely new community, and we feel that it is important to teach them to respect all property."

Mrs. Payne also explained, "In our drive for good community relations, we have been urging every child to attend Sunday school, and we have done rather nicely with them. The ministers cooperate with us; they come to all of the parents' meetings....The ministers come in often and have conferences. If any boy needs it, one of the ministers will come here and talk to him."

The overcrowding at School #159 was not alleviated until 1951 when Carter Godwin Woodson Elementary School # 160 opened at Seabury and Cherry Hill Roads. Mrs. Payne left School 159 to become Principal of School #160. Schools #160 and 180 were built on Baltimore City's cemetery for the poor—Potter's Field. Mrs. Lavania Booth was one of the participants in Dr. Breihan's history. She and her husband owned the dry cleaners in the Cherry Hill Shopping Center. She said she remembered seeing the undertaker picking up bones from the cemetery when it was being prepared to have the schools built on it.

According to Alberta Brown Campbell who attended School #160 when it first opened, "I remember seeing bones in the basement of the school. My class was making a paper mache dinosaur, and each day when we finished working on it, I had to take it to the basement to dry. I remember seeing the rounded mounds of dirt that the janitor said were graves." James said that children found bones on the playground. He said that school was closed for a week while the City continued to collect bones from the school grounds.

When I began kindergarten at School #159 in 1953, Mrs. Viola Wright was the principal. Mrs. Wright was light skinned with gray hair styled in a bob with a side part. She dressed very conservatively stylish and had a very regal bearing. She reminded me of Queen Elizabeth whom I had seen on TV and in movie newsreels. Mrs. Wright was a member of Delta Sigma Theta sorority, and was very socially active in the black community. She always treated us as though we were the smartest children in the world, and we wanted to meet her expectations of us. Mrs. Wright was a great advocate for her students and sought to give us every opportunity for exposure in the larger community of Baltimore City.

In the fall of 1954, one of the first grade teachers, Mrs. Janet Hughes, enrolled her daughter, also named Janet, in 159. Janet looked like a little white girl with hazel eyes and thick golden blonde braids down her back. The rumor was that Janet had gotten put out of St. Peter Claver School in west Baltimore because she was so bad. However, it turns out that her grandmother had suffered a heart attack and could no longer take care of her or walk her to school. Janet and I immediately became the best of friends, so much so that Mrs. Hughes asked my mother if Janet could come home with me after school until she got off from work. My mom said yes, and Janet became one of our family and a member of the Cherry Hill community.

Janet remembers, "Cherry Hill was a special place with kind and caring people, people who cared and nurtured students as well as their own children. They were wonderful, hardworking families who cared about their children getting an education. When I came back to teach at 159 in the 1990's as a master teacher, I brought a lot of fond memories with me."

By the time I was in the second grade, 159 was overcrowded again, and I spent the second grade in portables that had been set up on the playground. That overcrowding was not alleviated until Patapsco Elementary School #163 was built on Carver and Bridgeview Roads, right across the street from my house. When the school opened in January 1957, everyone on my block was transferred to 163 except me. My third grade teacher, Ms. Jacqueline Campbell (Hayman), was transferred to 163. Miss Campbell was one of several new, young teachers we got from Coppin State Teachers College. I loved Miss Campbell, and I wanted to go to the new school with her. Losing her made me physically ill, and for the first time since I started kindergarten, I missed a day of school. My mother explained to me that since I was a good student, Mrs. Wright wanted to keep me at 159.

When I was promoted to the fourth grade, I got another new teacher, Miss Bernice Tubman (Johnson) who was a descendant of Harriet

Tubman. Ms. Tubman was dark brown, petite, and very attractive. She was full of new ideas. Ms. Tubman started a Girl Scout Troop and a dance group. She picked students for special outings. I remember her taking a small group of us to the circus at the Fifth Regiment Armory and another time, to her home. Ms. Tubman left at the end of the year to get married and go to Germany with her husband who was in the military.

For fifth grade, I had Ms. Yvonne Bacoat (Willis), another product of Coppin who came from Winston Salem. Ms. Bacoat was in her second year at 159 when I got her, and she focused on teaching us to be ladies and gentlemen. She was beautiful with a soft southern accent that made you want to comply with her every wish. The boys were all smitten with her. Ms. Bacoat got married while she was teaching us and became Mrs. Willis. By the end of the school year, she was pregnant and left 159 to raise her family.

By the end of that school year, 1959, I found out that my family was going to have to leave public housing because my father's income exceeded the income limit. This became my mother's opportunity to get back to west Baltimore. I was devastated because I was being promoted to Mr. Clifton Ball's class, another Coppin export who was a very strict but excellent teacher, and I wanted to be in his class and graduate from 159. We moved to North Monastery Avenue in the Irvington section of southwest Baltimore so that Judy could attend the newly built Edmondson High School, the first comprehensive high school built in Baltimore City since WWII, and the first high school that would open in Baltimore City as an integrated high school with the first integrated faculty and staff.

Fortunately, one of the teachers who came to 159 from Coppin in the mid-1950s was my cousin, Isaac Harmon, who taught fifth and sixth grade. While we lived in Cherry Hill, Ike and his brother, David, who was a new teacher at 163, came to our house for my mom's home-cooked lunch every day. Ike and my mom worked out a plan for me to commute to with him to 159 for the sixth grade. Because of his kindness, I was able to stay and graduate from 159.

Mrs. Wright sent many of her students to junior high schools with the accelerated curriculum which allowed students to finish junior high school in two years instead of three. Several of us including Calvin and four of his classmates went in 1959. Rethia, Veronica, Yvette, and I went in 1960. Walter and Arthur were sent in 1961. I'm sure there were many other students at the other elementary schools who were also sent to this curriculum.

Nat Peacock also has wonderful memories of 159. "When my family moved to Cherry Hill from Fairmount Avenue and Baltimore Street in 1952, I was in the first grade and my teacher was Ms. Jones. I remember that first day at school because I met my first girl crush, Athena Gross. I also met my friend, Theodore Redfern, whom I suspect was Athena's crush. To this day, I have never told Theodore that I liked Athena. I enjoyed my time at 159 because all of my teachers were very nice. Mr. Milburn, the vice principal, used to carry a yard stick and hit you if you were in the hallway without a pass. My favorite teacher was Mr. Myers. I always looked at him as a father figure because he was the first male teacher I had. However, it was in Mr. Harmon's class in the 6th grade that I established friendships that lasted for many years. Mr. Harmon had three or four students that seemed to be his pets. I remember being jealous that I didn't seem to be one, but he always made me feel smart. I was in Mr. Harmon's class when my father passed, and I remember the special care he gave me at that time.

"I remember Mr. Harmon making me a safety patrolman. Before and after school my post was on Bridgeview Road where the elementary and junior high school kids traveled. My job was to keep the elementary kids from jay walking. However, the junior high kids would ignore me on purpose. It was funny because all the junior high kids knew my name because when it was time for me to leave my post, Mr. Harmon would yell, 'Peacock! It's time to go!' So the junior high kids would walk in the street and taunt me by yelling, 'Peacock! I'm in the street!' It was so funny, but you know I was scared of the big boys.

"Most of all, I remember our large playground and playing hop scotch, climbing the monkey pole, and playing duck duck goose. I can never forget May Day celebrations with everybody dressed up and the exhibition of some very colorful class projects ending with the wrapping of our May pole. Those were fun days."

Due to the pivotal role teachers played in the education of children in Cherry Hill, we called teachers to assist in telling this important story. We found ten teachers who taught in Cherry Hill schools between 1945and 1965 who volunteered to share their experiences. Each teacher completed a survey designed by Dr. Charity Welch, consisting of demographic information and several open-ended items to explain various aspects of their teaching experience in Cherry Hill. The majority taught in School # 159. Four of the teachers taught in Cherry Hill Junior High School #180.

Most teachers who taught in Cherry Hill were graduates of what is known today as Coppin State University. Coppin was founded in 1900 at what was then called the Colored High School (later named Douglass High School) on Pennsylvania Avenue by the Baltimore City School Board who initiated a one-year training course for the preparation of Black elementary school teachers. By 1902, the training program was expanded to a two-year Normal Department within the high school, and seven years later it was separated from the high school and given its own principal.

In 1926, this facility for teacher training was named Fanny Jackson Coppin Normal School in honor of the outstanding African-American woman who was a pioneer in teacher education. By 1938 the curriculum of the normal school was expanded to four years, authority was given for the granting of the Bachelor of Science degree, and the name of the Normal School was changed to Coppin Teachers College. In 1950, Coppin became part of the higher education system of Maryland under the State Department of Education, and renamed Coppin State Teachers College. Two years later Coppin moved to its present 38-acre site on West North Avenue. Coppin became Coppin State University in 2004 when all the State colleges were incorporated into the University of Maryland system.

Charity's survey revealed that all of the participating teachers lived outside of the Cherry Hill community, but they expressed a profound respect for the community and its residents. Mrs. Clustie Ford taught seventh- and ninth-grade math at School #180 from 1960 to 1962. She was impressed by the role parents played in the education of their children in this working class community. Mrs. Ford said, "Cherry Hill parents allowed teachers to visit their homes to discuss their children. Even if what you had to discuss was not favorable to the student, the parents supported the teacher and the teacher's recommendations."

Another teacher who taught at School #180 for nine years beginning in 1959, Jerrelle Foster Francois, stated,

"Parents taught students to respect teachers and education. Parents expected teachers to teach their children."

Delores Jessup began teaching at 180 in 1955 and stayed for ten years. She observed, "We were a close knit faculty—felt like family. We had picnics and socials together. We attended a funeral for one student. Towards the end of my tenure, the city had a negative opinion of the Cherry Hill community. However, they were a wonderful, caring people."

According to Isabel Dowdy, who taught a range of grades at School #159 for 25 years beginning in 1959, "It was not unusual to call on a parent to come in immediately to assist. Not unusual for a parent to bring lunch or stand at your door to ask if help was needed. The parents were most cooperative in every capacity. Cherry Hill was a good community to work with."

The teachers were also impressed by the quality of the students' home training. Ruth Harmon James graduated from Coppin in 1963 and served as a short-term substitute fourth grade teacher at 159. She notes, "The children were receptive, polite, and well mannered. They came to school prepared to learn with relatively few disciplinary situations."

Jacqueline Campbell Hayman, my third grade teacher who was transferred from School #159 to School #163, said, "The students were very bright, well behaved, and very competitive high achievers."

Calvin Thomas remembers the level of commitment that parents had toward the education of the children in Cherry Hill. "Since 159 did not have an auditorium, PTA meetings were held in the Community Center. I remember attending PTA meetings with my parents, and there would be standing room only. Parents would be standing all around the walls of the Center hearing the latest information about what was happening in the school system and meeting with the teachers about the progress of their children."

The Enoch Pratt Free Library, Baltimore City's public library, was an important resource for the education of children in Cherry Hill. Long before being a presence in Cherry Hill, the central Library had an award-winning Children's room that captured the imagination of all the children who passed through. The Children's Room had a pond of goldfish that mesmerized the children with their graceful maneuvering through the water. There were child sized tables, chairs and benches in groupings around the room with a corner of the room reserved for the story circle where the children could gather around the librarian as she selected a book to read to them. The library was open to everyone.

Teachers in Cherry Hill often assigned research projects and children went to the library after school to use the Encyclopedia and other text books to complete their projects. The library had been a fixture in the Cherry Hill community since 1951. Originally, the library was opened as the Cherry Hill Station, located at Giles and Cherry Hill Road. Then it became a branch and moved to its second location, 2700 Spellman Road in the Community Center in 1954.

Getting a library card was a milestone and privilege awarded to children who were able to demonstrate their ability to write their name on the library card. The shelves were sparsely stacked and some children read the same books several times. However, children enjoyed going to the library and sitting on the little stools to read a good book. In school children were taught the Dewey-Decimal System to learn how to locate specific books on the library shelves in school and in the public library.

The elementary schools included grades kindergarten through grade six. At School #159, each morning the school day began with a prayer, a Bible reading, and the pledge of allegiance to the flag followed by a patriotic song. Teachers taught reading in the morning using a series of books by Ginn and Company consisting of titles such as, *We Are Neighbors, On Cherry Street, Around the Corner* etc. The stories were all about the lives of white children and their families, and the books were often second-hand—passed on from white schools. Importantly, none of that made any difference—teachers taught reading and children enjoyed learning to read the stories.

The school curriculum consisted of Reading, Writing, Arithmetic, Handwriting, Spelling, English, Social Studies and Science. Each classroom had a trunk with musical instruments including bells, triangles, tambourines, xylophone and other instruments that children loved to play as they sang songs. Music, art, and physical education were important aspects of the curriculum. In warm weather, teachers took children to the playground for games such as Greek Dodge, Jump rope, Relay Races, etc. Other days, teachers allowed the children to play quiet games like Musical Chairs or Seven Up in the classroom.

The children also participated in good citizenship projects. There were annual charity drives like the March of Dimes or the Red Cross. Children literally collected dimes to bring in to fight polio, the chief function of the March of Dimes at that time. They were motivated to collect their pennies to give to the Red Cross. For each penny they donated, they received a Red Cross button. It got to be a competition of who wore the most of the colorful, fold-over, metal buttons. Every Monday after lunch they participated in Civil Defense Air Raid drills at which time a siren went off, and the children would scramble for a position under their desks to protect themselves in the event of a bombing. Every Wednesday the children would bring in their quarters to purchase U.S. Savings Stamps for their stamp books which eventually added up to the purchase of a U.S. Savings Bond. On April 21, 1955, School #159 served as one of the sites around the city to administer the Salk vaccine to first and second graders. Three doctors gave injections to 577 children.

Because there is so much emphasis placed on resource allocation in segregated schools, Charity sought to learn more from teachers about the resource allocation and support provided in Cherry Hill schools. She asked them, "What was your perception of the support from Baltimore

City Public Schools (BCPS) pertaining to the education of black students during the time you taught in Cherry Hill?"

Florine Austin Camphor, fifth grade teacher at School #159 from 1958 to 1964, said, "I felt that the BCPS was very concerned because when I asked for anything to help, it was there. I was able to get transportation to take the children on trips. The children I taught were very smart and wanted to learn. They wrote original stories and poems that they published in their school newspaper, *The 159 Journal*. Many of them have become national leaders."

Ms. Francois at School 180 chose to differ, saying "I thought there was little support for students in black communities in terms of educational resources. I compensated by using my own funds or searching out free materials."

Likewise, Catherine Dorsey, also of School #180, said, "I did not think our school received sufficient support. There were not enough books and supplies for the students. The students shared books and were not allowed to take them home. I bought a lot of supplies out of my pocket. In spite of lack of support with resources, I was proud to see my students excel in school, graduate from high school and college. Some received advanced degrees. I became very close to some families, participating in weddings, and attending baby showers and funerals."

Ms. Jessup adds, "There were insufficient poster boards and supplies for bulletin boards. We did not know that we did not have things. When I went into the city, I realized there were other things to ask for. Mrs. Jessup compensated by visiting the Art Department for help; purchasing supplies with her own money; visiting conventions, conferences, and soliciting assistance from publishing companies."

These responses provide some evidence that teachers in Cherry Hill faced some of the same resource allocation concerns that have been frequently reported in previous publications pertaining to segregated schools. The value of these responses is that they go further to shed light on the actions taken to compensate for those resource shortages. Teachers took advantage of opportunities to leverage resources through collaborations such as the School Music Committees, a group comprised of an educator from each school in the community. April 1955 marked the 31st observance of National Music Week and the schools in Cherry Hill celebrated with a week of musical events held at each of the schools and planned by the School Music Committees. Students proudly displayed their music talents and were treated to musical performances by local well known musicians.

Linda G. Morris

Many students at Cherry Hill Elementary School enrolled in half-day kindergarten at the age of 5 years old and attended school either a.m. or p.m. While at school, students in kindergarten learned social skills, how to dress for the weather, counting, poems, music, the calendar and seasons, and they had lots of play time. The day began with morning opening, discussion of the weather and calendar, songs, and stories read by the teacher. Later, the teacher passed out a snack consisting of 1/2 pint of white milk and graham crackers paid for with weekly milk money, a quarter, brought in by the children. When it was time to go home, the children were picked up by an older sibling or parent.

"Holidays were celebrated in schools, especially in the primary grades," said Margaret Turner who taught first grade at Schools 159 and 160 from 1951 to 1957. "Christmas, Halloween, and the seasons were all part of the curriculum and teachers enjoyed working with the children. Seasons were celebrated, and we would discuss how to be safe during the different times of the year. We focused on things that would protect the children like traffic and safety signs around the community."

Cherry Hill Elementary School provided a plethora of extra-curricular activities including instrumental music, dance, art, and singing. There were so many activities including Boy Scouts, safety patrols to assist with crossing the streets, Brownies and Girl Scout troops led by teachers who gave extra time in the evenings and on Saturdays to organize these activities. Students participated in school trips to the Walters Art Gallery, Fort McHenry, local television stations, the zoo and many other educational institutions that gave them broader exposure to the community at large. In 1952, a group of students dressed in their Sunday best visited the Afro American Newspaper officers to tour the building and observe the production of a modern newspaper. Students were always encouraged by their teachers to write and consequently, published the 159 Journal, a school newspaper filled with articles about school events as well as creative poetry and stories all written by students and typed by the school secretary, Mrs. Dorothy Hairston.

The value of field trips for students' learning was paramount for their broad exposure and intellectual growth. There has been an abundance of research pointing to the value of real life experiences for students' critical thinking and analytical skills. These trips, planned by teachers also gave students the opportunity to visit other parts of the city and state that they were learning about in their classes and may not otherwise have had an opportunity to visit. They often saw farms with cows and horses and were excited to see the animals that many had only read about in books.

Teachers also organized weekend trips to the bowling alley, park, or some other fun event. Students would use public transportation to meet teachers for a fun-filled afternoon. When students could not afford the cost of trips, teachers often used personal funds to cover the costs of the activity or purchase shoes, books or other items for students in need.

Although most teachers did not live in the community, it was not unusual to see teachers in the community visiting and checking on students during the weekend. Mrs. Wright was involved in many social groups, and she was a sorority member often involved in planning community activities. Teachers were relentless in their pursuit of excellence for each and every student. Their dedication did not end there. If needed, due to extenuating circumstances, children stayed at the teachers' homes. In the spring of 1954, a fire partially demolished a part of Cherry Hill Elementary School leaving 260 students in kindergarten, first and second grades without classroom space. Not even a fire could deter the dedicated teachers in Cherry Hill. Teachers, administrators and community immediately banded together to shift classes for these students to the Community Center for the remainder of the school year.

Cherry Hill Elementary School was a community school and as such it also served as the location for evening adult classes in Home Economics, and Arts and Crafts Courses, held Monday, Tuesday, and Wednesday evenings from 8 p.m. -10 p.m. The principal of the adult evening school was Mr. James P. Matthews. Adult learning classes were vital for families because they offered additional skills to pursue upward mobility in the form of better employment opportunities.

In the school system administration structure, segregated schools were a separate division led by Elmer A. Henderson, Director of Colored Schools. Mr. Henderson, born in 1887, was the son of a Methodist minister and "rose to prominence as one of Baltimore's leading educators in the first half of the twentieth century." Mr. Henderson often spoke publicly to convey official messages about the state of segregated or "colored" schools.

Concerns about school overcrowding and part time schedules at #159 and other Black schools across Baltimore City was an on-going point of discussion among the NAACP, the Board of School Commissioners, parents and other key stakeholders. As a result of overcrowding in segregated schools, students were forced to attend schools on shifts. In the latter part of the forties, because of overcrowding in primary grades, schools were described as "bulging at the seams." The greatest overcrowding situation occurred in Cherry Hill Elementary School with 1300 students, 24 part-time classes and 32 teachers in 1949. Since opening in 1946, the enrollment and faculty at Cherry Hill Elementary School had more than doubled.

While this enrollment situation was proliferating in Black communities, the NAACP argued that schools in White neighborhoods were under enrolled with seats that Black children could fill to ease the overcrowding in segregated schools. Filling those seats meant that children would have to attend school outside of their communities. The blatant reality was that many Black parents did not want their children to attend schools outside of their safe and welcoming community. In addition, part-time schedules often placed a burden on working parents with young children being assigned different schedules from siblings. Although part-time schedules were not ideal, teachers, determined to impart knowledge and not be discouraged, continued without interruption.

Mrs. Margaret Turner, a first-grade teacher who taught using the part time schedule, recalled the opportunities it provided for communication and collaboration between two teachers sharing the same classroom. Mrs. Turner said, "It was tight, but it gave teachers an opportunity to share resources and ideas." She recalled how teachers intuitively respected each other's space. Essentially, they made the best of the situation at hand.

On the afternoon of May 17, 1954, United States Supreme Court Chief Justice Earl Warren announced the Supreme Court's decision in Brown v. Board of Education. History was made when Warren read the following words: "Does segregation of children in public schools solely on the basis of race, even though the physical facilities and other 'tangible' factors may be equal, deprive the children of the minority group of equal educational opportunities? We believe that it does." Warren then read the following historical words into the record: "We conclude-unanimously— that, in the field of public education, the doctrine of 'separate but equal' has no place. Separate educational facilities are inherently unequal." The NAACP viewed desegregation as the right of African-Americans as individuals to have legal access to white institutions on the same basis as any other citizen. In the 1955 re-arguments in the remedial phase of Brown, the NAACP attempted to persuade the Supreme Court to mandate specific deadlines for desegregation of schools.

As it turns out, the most important school policies that impact school desegregation are housing policies, and efforts to make changes have been merely perfunctory, at best. The landmark decision marked the end of legal segregation, yet little changed in public housing in Baltimore. The HABC replaced its official segregated policy with one of "freedom of choice." How could such a process work to achieve racial integration in 1954?

Dr. Charlene Coleman Griffin, who began teaching at School #159 in 1956, said, "Three teachers from our school were asked to transfer to a school where the students and staff were predominantly white, in an effort toward integration. Two agreed and were transferred. The other one asked to remain with her school and children."

Judy remembers being one of several fifth graders bused from School #159 to Westport Elementary School #225. "I was in the fourth grade at 159 when the decision came down. My mom sat me down and explained to me that I would be going to a new school. This was already the third elementary school I had attended. Mom told me that the NAACP and Thurgood Marshall had won the right for black children to go to school with white children. I didn't know why that should be any different, and I trusted that mom would not make a bad decision for me. Mom was especially proud of Mr. Marshall because he was a Baltimorean and had attended Douglass High School, her alma mater, a few years before she graduated. Mom told me that I was going to ride a bus to Westport Elementary School #225. I took it all in stride.

Westport was a white community north of Cherry Hill. We caught the bus at 159 for the 10 minute ride. If we got to Westport early, we would go to the store on the corner and buy penny candy. The children seemed all right, and we got along fine. I think the teacher's name was Mrs. Wine, and I remember her being firm but fair. She was very good at history, and I remember her making you feel like you were there.

The bus driver always admonished us to be at the bus stop on time, or we would be left behind. One day I missed the bus and had to walk home. I had a few pennies, and I stopped at the store, bought some candy and started walking to Cherry Hill. It didn't take long at all. Sometimes other children would miss the bus, and they would wave at us as the bus drove by, not seeming to care that they weren't on the bus. Now I knew how they felt."

Gwen had quite a different experience with busing. "I was bussed from 160 to 225 in the fourth and fifth grades. We had to get up an hour earlier and walk up the hill to 160 to catch the school bus leaving a brand new school to attend an old school that smelled like mold. We had new text books at 160, but 225 had old books. One day, my fourth grade teacher, Mrs. Fiorello, told me to tell my mother that she was looking for someone to clean her house. Not knowing any better, I went home and told my mother. The next day, my mother sent me back to school with a message for Mrs. Fiorello. I told her, 'My mother is looking for someone to clean our house too.' I was so glad to get back to 160 for the sixth grade and be back with my friends."

In 1959, Dr. Houston R. Jackson, assistant superintendent, articulated a plan to minimize part-time classes that would result in larger class sizes. In sharing that plan, Dr. Jackson pointed out that experience had shown a reduction in learning when class size was larger. He went on to state that the situation for the following year looked brighter due to a system-wide plan that included transporting (busing) students from Cherry Hill Elementary School to Mt. Winans Elementary School No.156 in the adjacent black public housing project. In his statement, Dr. Jackson stated, "There isn't an elementary school in the city more beautiful or better equipped than the new Mt. Winans," which consisted of a gym-auditorium, cafeteria, library, modern furniture, lavatories adapted to the students' size, and a very large paved play area. Would those beautiful features be enough for Black students bused from Cherry Hill to feel welcome, comfortable and supported at school? By September 1959, the school board announced its plans to ease overcrowding with the approval of an addition to School # 159 to include 14 new classrooms, a multi-purpose room with stage, teachers' work room, and gym and increased storage. Also, the last elementary school in Cherry Hill, Arundel Elementary School #164, opened in 1960.

The Cherry Hill community can proudly boast about the success of many of its students who, as children, had no real understanding of the inequities that existed in the schools they attended. These students' success stories contradict the widespread notion that those who attended segregated schools were less than or not capable of being competitive outside of their own communities. To the contrary, teachers showed concern for students and provided an education that prepared them to be competitive while giving them the confidence to break through barriers placed in their pathways. Positive messages and support received from educators, family, and community allowed students to successfully navigate the educational system to become leaders in their communities and the world. The Cherry Hill community cared deeply about its children, and adults wrapped arms around children to protect them.

The current principal of 159, Tracey Weems Garrett, is a third generation Cherry Hill former resident. Tracey attended 159 in the 1970s. After graduating from 159, her mother and step-father, who was in the Air Force, whisked her off to Maine where she attended junior high school. Tracey said, "That was a very lonely time for me. Although the children were nice, my academics suffered from me trying to fit in. I was the only black child placed in the top class due to my great report card from 159. So I intentionally didn't perform my best to get into the class that had other black kids. It was very hard to leave such a close-knit, supportive community, but when I look back, I'm glad for having experiences outside of my community.

"I find that even today, some Cherry Hill parents are very reluctant to let their children leave Cherry Hill for experiences outside of their community, such as attending out of zone high schools. One of our school's goals is to prepare children for college and careers in the 21st century. That's why it's important for them to have composite scores that will allow them to choose among the top performing high schools in Baltimore City. We want them to be able to compete globally and their high school experience will be crucial to their future success. More of our parents are now on board with their child attending high school outside of the community. I share with my scholars often the numerous successful people from the same community in which they live, including me, and tell them they can be successful too!"

Today, Cherry Hill #159 and Arundel #164 are both currently under renovation and construction to provide 21st Century School Buildings for the children in the Cherry Hill Community. School #164 will have grades pre-K through two with several child care and early childhood amenities, and 159 will have grades three through eight. School #180, the junior high school, will become a high school. The new schools are scheduled to open their doors in the fall of 2018.

7.

Real Affordable Health Care

Cherry Hill was fortunate enough to have really dedicated and compassionate medical and dental professionals. We had three doctors, two of whom lived in Cherry Hill, and a dentist who also lived there. The doctors and our dentist were among the first to purchase homes in Cherry Hill Village. The doctors provided 24-hour care because if we called them, they would come no matter what time it was. If we couldn't afford to pay them, they still treated us. They were all affiliated with the Baltimore City Health Department clinics.

Dr. and Mrs. Jerry Conrad Luck were among the first home owners in Cherry Hill Village. They bought two row houses at 425 and 427 Swale Avenue—425 and the upper floor of 427 being their residence and the first floor of 427 being Dr. Luck's office. Dr. Luck was born in Danville, Virginia, and moved to Washington, DC, where he graduated from Howard University. He received his medical degree from Meharry University Medical School in Nashville, Tennessee, one of only two medical schools (the other being Howard University Medical School) training black doctors. Dr. Luck did his internship and residency at the Homer G. Phillips Hospital in St. Louis, Missouri.

Mrs. Gertrude Carlock Luck, known as Trudy, was born in Pittsburgh and raised in Cincinnati. She attended Meharry Medical College School of Nursing, and she served with the Army Nurse Corps before receiving her nursing degree. She accepted a nursing position at Homer G. Phillips, and on December 26, 1944, she and Dr. Luck were married. They moved into their Cherry Hill Village home in 1945. Mrs. Luck served as Dr. Luck's nurse until they started their family of two sons, Jerry, Jr., and Larry. Mrs. Luck was very active in St. Veronica's Church and in the community.

Dr. and Mrs. Renold B. and Ruth White Lighston bought homes at 501 and 503 Cherry Hill Road. Like the Lucks, they were also newlyweds. Dr. Lighston received his undergraduate degree at Lincoln University in Pennsylvania in 1938, graduated from Howard University Medical School, and completed his internship and residency at Harlem Hospital before moving to Cherry Hill with his bride 1945. Mrs. Lighston worked in the school system as a counselor at Cherry Hill Jr. High School and was a member of the Delta Sigma Theta sorority. Dr. Lighston had his office in 501 and the family, including his children Renold III, Heber, Susan, and Ruth, and a live-in housekeeper, lived at 503 and on the second floor of 501.

Dr. John Sarjent Braxton, Jr., was born and raised in Philadelphia. He graduated from Central High School there in 1939 and went to Lincoln University in Oxford, Pennsylvania, for two years. He came out of school to join the Army, but he returned to Lincoln and earned his bachelor's degree in 1948. Dr. Braxton attended Howard University Medical College of Medicine, received his medical degree in 1952, and completed his internship and residency at Philadelphia General Hospital. Dr. Braxton established his practice in Cherry Hill in 1954, and his wife, Joslyn L. Ferrell, a registered nurse and formerly a Morgan State College nurse, worked with him in his practice on Terra Firma Road in the Waterview Homes development. However, they did not live in Cherry Hill.

Our dentist, Dr. Edward McDaniels, Jr., was born in Baltimore and was a graduate of Morgan State College. He graduated from Howard University School of Dentistry in 1944. Dr. McDaniels was a captain in the Army toward the end of WWII. He came to Cherry Hill in 1947 and purchased a house at 518 Bridgeview Road, where he lived and had his office. In 1949, he married Bernice T. Mitchell who also graduated from Morgan and was a dietician at the Henryton Tuberculosis Sanitarium. The McDaniels did not have any children, but they were very active in the community being members of many charitable and social organizations. Mrs. McDaniels was a member of the Delta Sigma Theta sorority, the Moles, and the Chums. Dr. McDaniels was a member of Chi Delta Mu, his professional fraternity, and Omega Psi Phi. They were always in the *Afro* for their charitable events.

In 1950, Baltimore City started a school dental program to provide constructive and preventive treatment to students in the kindergarten and first grade and expanding the grade levels as these children got older. Mayor D'Alesdanro opened the first school dental suite in Canton Elementary School. In 1953, a dental suite was opened in the newly constructed Carter G. Woodson School #160 in Cherry Hill. Dr. McDaniels was on the staff of the Baltimore City Health Department's Bureau of Dental Care and provided dental services to all the elementary schools in Cherry Hill. Baltimore City was one of the first and largest cities to add fluoride to its water supply in November 1952. Thus, the City was on the cutting edge of pediatric dentistry and our own Dr. McDaniels was a charter member of this program.

Those of us who attended school #159, hated to see Dr. McDaniels' Cadillac pull up in front of our school. That meant that 3 or 4 unlucky children would be called to the office and told they were going with Dr. McDaniels for their dental check-ups. Dr. McDaniels would put us in the back seat of his car, drive us up the street to his office, and take care of our dental issues. I can remember going in the second and third grades. We all got in Dr. McDaniel's car with terror-stricken faces—some with tears running down our cheeks. We would walk reluctantly into his office—no one wanting to be first. He would call the first child into his dental suite, the door would close, and the terror level rose even more as we listened to our classmates crying and Dr. McDaniels admonishing them to stop crying and open their mouths. When it was your turn, all you could do is look at the victims who had gone in before you and know it wasn't going to be a good experience. After all students were treated, Dr. McDaniels packed us into the back seat of his Cadillac and dropped us back at school.

The students at School #160 experienced the same terror in their newly built school with its own dental suite. Gwen remembers, "Panic could be seen on my classmates' faces when our teacher would call their names to let them know that they were going to see Dr. McDaniels. Lucky for me and my siblings, when my mother took us to his office, we had each other to cling to while praying we would not be the first one called. My brothers would start crying and we would join in the chorus crying too. It was a nightmare."

Our doctors were phenomenal. They could diagnose us without extensive medical testing and medical equipment. They gave us great follow-up care such that we did not have to be hospitalized a lot. Each practice had its own personality. Dr. Lighston's office had a receptionist who kept track of the patients and the office business. Dr. Lighston also had a pharmacy in the room behind his office, and he often mixed medical remedies. Houston remembers how his mother helped Dr. Lighston make cough syrup.

"We kids would pick buckets and buckets of the tiny black rum cherries for which Cherry Hill was named. My mother had some clay crocks, and she would fill up the crocks with the cherries, add a particular type of yeast, sugar, and water and sit the mixture in the cool dark basement to ferment. Around Christmas, she would strain the cherry meat and pits out using cheese cloth and let the strained liquid sit for a week or so. She would syphon off the top quarter and bottle it up for table wine. She would put the remaining liquid in another clay crock that sealed tightly and had a hole in the top of the lid in which she would insert a copper tube that went to a clear glass container. As this liquid fermented, the alcohol would drip into the glass container. By spring, she would deliver the purest batch to Dr. Lighston. The alcohol that was delivered to Dr. Lighston was mixed in his lab with other ingredients and dispensed as cough syrup."

Dr. Braxton's wife worked with him as his nurse, and they treated patients together—even doing house calls together. Dr. Luck had more of a laid back practice. There was no one in his office but him. He had morning and evening hours. Patients walked down to his office and just got in line about a half hour before the scheduled hour. At the appointed time, Dr. Luck would open the door, with his ever-present cigarette dangling from his lips, and we would file in remembering our own order. Amazingly everyone remembered his or her place in the line because there was never any question about who should go in when Dr. Luck said, "Next." No one ever complained about the cigarette. He charged $3 for a visit from the time he opened the office into the late 1960s.

If there were tragedies in or near the area, our doctors would be called. One such occasion was June 1949, Dr. Luck was called to the scene of a land slide at the foot of the clay cliffs. Three young Cherry Hill residents had been playing there when clay and sand shifted to cause a cave in. Two witnesses who were walking along the road observed the boys playing in a hollowed-out section up an embankment shortly before the earth above them gave way. Sixteen firemen from Curtis Bay and two other engine companies, several police officers, and many volunteers dug frantically for 15 minutes trying to get the pair out, but it was not soon enough to save the brothers. Dr. Luck pronounced two of the boys, Robert and Al Smith, brothers, 7 and 3 years old, dead at the scene. Another 3 year old, James Weems, was lifeless as he was dug out, but after 15 minutes of resuscitation efforts, he was revived. Those wondrous red clay cliffs turned deadly—many times.

There were always rumors of quicksand, whirlpools, or other unsettled land swallowing people up. According to Linda, two children got caught up in quicksand somewhere in the area behind Roundview Road near Ascension Street. Linda said, "It was a brother and sister taking a short cut home from school. The sister was running slightly ahead of her brother and ran into the quicksand. She of course started yelling and screaming, and her brother raced to save her. He went in trying to pull her up, and he began to sink. Other children were coming home from school, saw them in distress and tried to help. They tried to form a human chain to get to them, but the brother sank before they could get to him. By the time the fire department arrived, both the brother and sister were pronounced dead when their bodies were brought up."

In the late 1940s, Baltimore's hospitals were segregated and black women could not get obstetric services at most of them. The University of Maryland Hospital would send interns into the black community to train them to deliver babies at home. Johns Hopkins had a colored maternity ward. Provident Hospital, the only black hospital in the city, was also a source for maternity care. However, Baltimore City Hospitals, located on the far northeastern corner of Baltimore City, was the primary public hospital for the poor, and as such, many black women, including my mother, delivered their babies there. Dr. Luck, Dr. Lighston, and Dr. Braxton all had privileges at Baltimore City Hospitals and Provident Hospital. Dr. Luck also ran the Cherry Hill Well Baby Clinic from 1946 to 1955. The clinic was subsequently named for him.

Darleen McClain-Smith was born in Cherry Hill and continues to reside there. She was born at 2835 Spelman Road, moved to 2829 Spelman Road when she was 2, moved to 2809 Windwood Court when she was 7, moved to 2910 Round Road at 22, moved to 2500 Giles Road at 28, and has resided at 3442 Round Road for the past 20 years. Darlene said, "My mother and father, Rosetta and Theodore McClain, moved to Cherry Hill when they were pregnant with me, after my two older brothers, Teddy and Stevie, were born. Dr. Luck delivered me, my sister Rosetta, and my brother Gregory at home. My siblings Henry, Patrice, and Jacqueline were born in hospitals. Dr. Luck was always there, any hour of the day or night, when we needed him. I remember when my baby finger was dislocated, and Dr. Luck set it. It's still crooked. When I look at it, I always remember Dr. Luck with a cigarette dangling from his mouth as he worked."

Wes shares his most memorable experience of going to Dr. Luck, "I was about nine years old, and not being one to always listen to my mother,

I was playing with the hot iron (on the ironing board) after she left the room and instructed me to just stay seated in the assigned chair in which she had placed me. As she was away doing something else for a few brief minutes, I somehow managed to reach the top of the ironing board and touch the iron which then dropped onto my left arm in the area of the muscle region.

"The pain and my resulting screams brought my mother running back into the room. She immediately administered first aid with first butter to stop the pain and then a healing cream to get rid of the mark. I got over the pain, as well as my mother scolding me for not listening to her, and the wound seemed to be healing well. Three days later, the blister that developed was about to heal, when I suddenly scraped it. This resulted in a liquid discharge that led to a thinly exposed skin area which days later became inflected, and I had a horrible looking scab on the burn area.

"My mother took me to see Dr. Luck. I vividly recall him pulling back my short sleeve shirt that I was wearing on a normally hot summer mid-July day, and he commented to me, 'Oh we can take care that.' Before I heard another word come out of his mouth, he took a cotton ball and abruptly removed the scab from my arm, exposing pure white skin and cells mixed with dots of blood on the surface. Between the shock from the pain, the intriguing look of the exposed surface as I starred at it, and the matter-of-fact routine treatment by Dr. Luck, I experienced a jolt to my system that stays with me, even after more than 50 years. The scar that the healed wound left still exists as a perfect circle on my left arm muscle from Dr. Luck's removal of the scab. Dr. Luck healed my burn and left me scarred for life—figuratively and literally. Yet he did not damage or traumatize me in any way—emotionally or physically."

Dr. Luck was a very no nonsense kind of doctor. He didn't have time to coddle you because he always had twenty or so folks ready to take your place in his waiting room. I always knew that even though I was sick going in, like a miracle, I would be well coming out. When I was about seven, I was in my second tap dance class at the Community Center. My mom didn't want me dancing, but my dad did. She was really upset when she had to put taps on a pair of my Sunday patent leather shoes which was cheaper than buying tap shoes. There I was tapping in a circle, holding hands with the other dancers when I slipped and fell forward on my face onto the concrete floor. I split my bottom lip, and it was bleeding badly. The instructor got my belongings and ushered me out the door with one of the moms who lived in my area.

I cried and bled the whole seven-block walk home. When my mom saw me standing there with my lip bleeding, she thanked the mom who brought me home, and rushed upstairs to get dressed so that we could walk down to Dr. Luck's office. As we walked, I was still bleeding and crying, especially after my mom said that I would probably have to have stitches. I didn't know what they were, but they sounded painful. We got to Dr. Luck's office, and when it was our turn, we went in. I remember Dr. Luck looking at my lip, with his signature cigarette dangling from his lip, and he got up and went into his cabinet. He came back with what looked like a perfume atomizer, and he sprayed some powdery stuff on my lip. Whatever it was, it stopped the bleeding, and best of all, he didn't give me any stitches. From that day on, Dr. Luck was my hero.

Dr. Lighston was affiliated with the Health Department's pediatric clinic. In the summer of 1946, Dr. Lighston was lauded in the *Afro* for delivering triplets, all boys, unassisted in an East Baltimore residence. He worked on one baby trying to get it to breath for more than an hour, and then he put the babies in his car, in the days before seatbelts and car seats, and drove them to Johns Hopkins Hospital where they were put on incubators. Dr. Lighston also delivered Arthur and Houston Murphy at their Round Road home. Dr. Lighston was part of a medical delegation sent to Haiti in 1960 to help reorganize the Haitian medical system by the Medical International Cooperation Organization (MEDICO). This organization was hoping to use this effort to model future medical interventions in the newly independent countries of Africa.

As late as 1959, our doctors were still delivering babies at home in Cherry Hill. According to Leonard Hamm, former Baltimore City Police Commissioner, "I remember Dr. Braxton delivering my brother Daniel (Jerry) in the evening of January 3, 1959. My father could not get my mother to the hospital, and he called Dr. Braxton. Dr. Braxton came to our house at 3303 Round Road and delivered my brother in my mother and father's bed. There were five other children already in the home, and we were excited—not at all fearful. My father seemed confident as did Dr. Braxton. My mother did not appear to be in any distress. Dr. Braxton respected our home, as humble as it was. After the delivery he announced, 'You have a new baby brother.' I don't think my father paid him at the time."

One of the worst times for those of us who went to Dr. Luck was when he had to leave for two years to fulfill his military obligation in April 1956. The Cherry Hill Coordinating Council, an umbrella organization of Cherry Hill clubs, churches, associations, and merchants, gave him a going-away testimonial at the Community Center to show how much we appreciated him. Over 400 residents attended the program which had music, and presentations of notes of appreciation from most of the churches and clubs in Cherry Hill, and ice cream donated by the Cherry Hill Shopping Center Segal Pharmacy. The group presented Dr. Luck with a set of luggage and gave Mrs. Luck an orchid and a hand bag. We truly missed him for the two years he was gone. When he came back, it was just as though he had not missed a beat.

Thanks to our doctors and dentist, no one in Cherry Hill lacked for treatment. They were family to us, and I know they felt the same about us. Patricia Pinkney Gaither relates how Dr. Lighston treated her younger brother, Thomas Pinkney, for chronic and debilitating asthma. Patricia said, "There were no nebulizers or inhalers then, and emergency injections were essential. No matter what the hour, Dr. Lighston was there when Thomas needed him."

Patricia remembers Mrs. Lighston being like a mother to her and the children she counseled at Cherry Hill Jr. High School #180. "Renard Lighston, Jr., and I were among the first seven black children—and the only ones from Cherry Hill—to be accepted into the Johns Hopkins University Summer Program for Gifted and Talented Children. Mrs. Lighston drove us every day and picked us up. We would have a picnic lunch at one of the park areas, either on campus or in the Leakin park area. Sometimes she would cross the street from the campus to buy us ice cream cones. I don't think either of us realized that she was sheltering and protecting us from the overt racism and danger that was prevalent. She could not protect us from it in the classrooms, but thankfully the only physical attacks were occasional shoves from behind, people trying and often tripping us, and teachers refusing to call on us."

Rethia, a retired school nurse, says she only now can appreciate the value our medical and dental professionals added to our community and our lives. "As the child of a single mother who was a domestic worker, there were many times I got sick and there was no money for a doctor. Because of them, I received the care that I needed whether my mother could pay or not. There were no 'Pay at the time services are rendered' signs in their offices to make us feel like we would be denied care. I now understand how remarkably kind and compassionate they were as practitioners and members of our community, with families of their own to support and care for, they offered needed health care to thousands in the Cherry Hill community for decades. Without their service, jobs would have been lost, days from school would have been missed, but most importantly, lives would have been devastated. They were there when many of us took our first breath; comforted us when we were suffering with TB, STD's, polio, diphtheria, injuries, tooth decay and many ailments that we did not understand. They held our hands and the hands of our parents, reassuring us that all would be well. They were our voice within the medical community, representing our community interest on the health department board. Those of us that were inspired by them and therefore followed in their footsteps to a career in health care now know and appreciate their many sacrifices."

8.

The Murphy Family

Every town has its prominent families, and one of the most prominent families in Baltimore is the Murphys. They are held in high esteem because they have fought for equality, equity, and justice for black Baltimore long before our generation was born. The Murphys are black Baltimore's Kennedys. As mentioned earlier, John H. Murphy, Sr. founded the *Afro-American Newspapers*, and his son, Dr. George B. Murphy, was involved in the development of Cherry Hill, being the first black commissioner on the board of the Housing Authority of Baltimore City. Dr. Murphy's son, William H. Murphy, Sr. (who in 1970 became the first black judge elected to the Baltimore City Municipal Court), moved his young family to Cherry Hill because, as Judge Murphy's late son Arthur noted at his father's funeral, "He wanted his children to be raised with real people and not among the aspiring middle class of Baltimore. He loved Cherry Hill and hated to leave it."

Lawyer Murphy, as Judge Murphy was called in the early years in Cherry Hill, made history as the third black law student to be accepted into the University of Maryland Law School. However, it wasn't without a fight. In February 1939, he sought admittance to the Law School after graduating from Oberlin College. The University of Maryland Law School is the same school that denied Supreme Court Justice Thurgood Marshall admittance. In keeping with its segregationist stance, University of Maryland President H. C. Byrd sought to deny Murphy admission after having denied admission to two other black law students that he was forced subsequently to admit. The first law student, Donald G. Murray, and the

NAACP attorneys Charles Houston, Thurgood Marshall, and William Gosnell—the same team that won Brown V. Board of Education—sued the University and won admittance for Mr. Murray on the grounds that the State had not provided separate but equal opportunity for blacks to attend professional schools. The University was forced to admit Mr. Murray while it developed a way to provide separate but equal graduate education. Byrd's solution was to set up a scholarship fund to provide blacks who wanted graduate education opportunity to attend out of state schools, a remedy codified by the state legislature. The Maryland Commission on Higher Education was established for the purpose of administering scholarships of up to $10,000 to send black graduate students out of state.

On September 6, Byrd contacted Mr. Murphy, after Murphy's many attempts to contact the school, and Byrd offered to pay his full tuition to Harvard Law School to avoid having to admit him. Byrd told Murphy that the University would turn its plant over to private management rather than admit more "colored students" to its law school. It was only when Murphy threatened to bring suit with the NAACP that Byrd relented and admitted Murphy to the law school.

Mr. Murphy was preparing to enter his third year of law school when he was drafted into the army in September 1941. He served his country as an Army intelligence officer in North Africa and attained the rank of second lieutenant. When he completed his service, he came back to Baltimore and completed law school. Mr. Murphy met his future wife, Madeline Wheeler of Wilmington, Delaware, at a dance at Temple University where Ms. Wheeler attended, and they married while he was in his third year of law school. After briefly living in Delaware and Chicago, they moved to Baltimore in 1945. The couple spent a year living in Turner's Station, a newly built Negro war housing development in northeast Baltimore County, before moving to public housing in Cherry Hill in 1947. At that time, they had two of their five children, William H. (Billy) Murphy, Jr., 5, and Madeline, 3.

Shortly after Lawyer Murphy moved to Cherry Hill, the home owners in the private housing were beginning to experience complaints about the construction of their homes and sought him out for advice. According to an account by Mrs. Murphy in the Breihan Cherry Hill history, "had one person come to him as a client and then came to find out it was all these people in the same place who needed a lawyer also. He said, 'I tell you what to do. You get all these people on the block together … and I'll charge them a dollar a piece. We'll have [a] sort of class action suit against the builder.'" Suit was filed against The Myerberg Company, one of the developers who constructed the private homes, and the officers of Cherry Hill Village, Inc., an affiliated enterprise. Ten indictments were leveled against them, and in 1949, they were found guilty of 90 housing code violations. Lawyer Murphy and the home owners formed The Cherry Hill Protective Association, the first of many grass roots organizations that sprouted up to protect Cherry Hill citizens.

Shortly thereafter, the Murphys built the iconic brown bungalow on the hill at 3217 Round Road, and the family expanded to include sons Arthur and Houston, and daughter Laura. Mrs. Murphy decided to deliver two of her children, Arthur and Houston, at home rather than to have them at one of Baltimore's segregated hospitals. She delivered her other children at Provident Hospital, the city's black hospital. Perhaps it was this injustice that called Mrs. Murphy to become the crusader for social and economic justice that she became for Cherry Hill. Everyone in Cherry Hill knew of the Murphys and where they lived. Whenever residents got into legal trouble, they sought out Mr. Murphy. Otherwise, they sought the guidance of Mrs. Murphy for help to find resources to better their living conditions. The names William and Madeline Murphy are laced tightly throughout the history of Cherry Hill.

Madeline Murphy Rabb, now a jewelry designer living in Chicago, reflects on her parents, "Arthur was right. Our parents had an intolerance and disdain for superficial black bourgeois values. Before moving to Cherry Hill, we lived in Turner Station in what was called Negro War Housing. My father was a veteran, and he had an interest in buying a house in Cherry Hill because it was a new, safe, affordable community. However, before moving into our home on Round Road, we lived in public housing on Sethlow Road. My parents were dedicated to making a difference in Cherry Hill.

"Another reason they stayed was that our father was a saver, extremely frugal (to everyone's despair) and insisted on living beneath his means. By staying in Cherry Hill, he could afford a large house on a big plot of land, have a big garden, annual family vacations and pay for all five of his children's educations. I'm absolutely sure that a more upscale community would not have tolerated my father's obsessive devotion to building a wall that took almost 30 years to complete, unaided and from the labor of his own hands and of course of the hands of my siblings and I."

There was a strong sense of community in Cherry Hill where everyone looked after one another's children. We would walk all over Cherry Hill by ourselves. I used to love selling *Afros*. I took over Billy's paper route one summer, and got rid of all the non-paying customers. When he returned, he had a fully paid up paper route. I think Billy just liked getting out of the house and had fun with his paper route. His dear customers were stunned by me, who at a young age was a no nonsense business woman and insisted on being paid—no pay no paper! Billy loved to tell me how happy his customers where when he returned from camp that summer. He said they told him, 'Madeline is mean!'

"We would walk to the Hill Theater in the Cherry Hill Shopping Center on Saturdays. I remember when I was about 12 years old, I was walking by myself to the A&P grocery store in the Shopping Center. I passed a white man with his car door open exposing himself. I ran away unharmed. I must have been pretty fearless, because I continued on to the A&P."

Houston Murphy shared how important his paper route was to him, and the role it played with his relationship to the larger community. "When I turned 10, I was initiated into the fraternity that all young Murphy boys must belong—starting and maintaining an *Afro American Newspaper* route. Initially, I was anything but enthusiastic about having a paper route. I became even less so when my late older brother, Arthur, begrudgingly seeded my route with nine of his most delinquent customers plus one customer he didn't like—Mrs. Patterson at 917 Bridgeview Road. The nine delinquent customers were scattered on various Cherry Hill streets close to our home. I remember all of their names to this day. You might wonder how or why I would remember the names of a few newspaper customers from over 50 years ago. The truth is that not only do I remember these customers' names, but I remember over half of the names of my 250 plus customers I eventually serviced. They were loyal customers to me until I quit the newspaper route in 1969.

Mr. and Mrs. Murphy were deeply entrenched in the service of the Cherry Hill community. When the boys got into trouble, parents would take their sons to Lawyer Murphy for his advice on getting them through the criminal justice system as unscathed as possible. Mrs. Murphy was a community organizer who worked at the Presbyterian Church and offered literacy classes, rummage sales and taught bible school. She was also a notary, so residents came to her to get their documents notarized inexpensively—for a dime.

Houston remembers, "Back in the 60's, Cherry Hill was probably one of the friendliest, quietest, safest, places in the City of Baltimore. You *never* heard gunfire, rarely heard angry shouting. Black policemen, school teachers, security guards and just about any other profession lived in Cherry Hill. It was not unheard of for me to start my Friday route at whatever time the newspapers arrived (anywhere between 3pm to 7pm or even not until the next day) and wind up coming home anywhere between 7pm to as late as 11pm. Having the newspapers arrive early and ready for delivery was always a game of chance. The things that could delay the papers arriving were bad weather, late breaking news that the editor wanted in the Friday edition, the printing presses breaking down, the delivery vehicle breaking down or any number of other problems. Mr. Evans, my route manager, would deliver them as soon as possible. However no matter what time they arrived, the newspapers always had to be delivered.

"Every Friday during school year, as I came home from school, I always wondered if the newspapers had arrived yet. During summer vacation, all my friends knew that on Tuesdays and Fridays, I had other responsibilities. They could come along with me while I delivered newspapers if they wanted, but it was clear that I wasn't giving them any of the money I collected (although I sometimes sprung for Royal Crown Colas from the Daddy Logan truck). They especially knew that I wasn't doing anything else with them while I was selling newspapers. If there was an exception, it was my best friend, Steven Gary Lewis. If I was Huckleberry Finn, Steven Gary Lewis was Tom Sawyer. He was my partner in crime and mischief, a real charmer, and the only friend who could control my dog. If he and I fought, my dog would just jump around us but not intervene.

"There were a number of reasons why my parents rarely worried about me being out late on Friday. First, I had a really loyal and well-trained dog, King Lear, who never left my side and wouldn't even let my father beat me, let alone almost anyone else. Second, during at least the first two years, my parents got regular telephone updates from some of my customers. Lastly, they (mostly) trusted me and Steven and, more importantly, our neighbors and neighborhood. I started out conscientious about work and have not changed. I tell people that selling newspapers was my gateway drug to harder work.

"I really grew to look forward to newspaper days. Each newspaper day was new and different. Would Mrs. Brown be cooking chitterlings or croaker for dinner? Would Doris Dunham be home (I had a crush on her, among others)? Would the Baker boys or David across the street from the Bakers (elementary school classmates) be in good moods or bad? Would the Daddy Logan truck (a mobile grocery store) be on Spellman road by the time I hit that part of the route? Would Steven Gary Lewis join me for part of my route? What dog would be loose who'd either want to get in a fight with King, or worse, was King in heat (leash time)?

"The majority of my remembrances are good, but some of them are bad. I lost classmates and neighbors to the Viet Nam war. Some who went to war, survived, and came back were psychologically maimed. Some came back maimed as well as addicted to heroin. When I gave up my newspaper route in 1969 before going off to college, I had to divide the route between four kids whom I chose. I had kids that looked up to me who would sometimes follow me while I delivered my newspapers. It was from these kids I chose my successors. Saying good bye to all of my customers for the last time was really bitter sweet. Bitter because, after having them as customers for years, I would miss them terribly. Leaving was sweet because I was moving away from home to something new. That last week, I cried, and some of my customers cried, too. I kept in touch with many of my former customers and some of their children. Every time I came home from college, I would find one of my mentees and walk the route with him."

9.

Building Community

The success of the early Cherry Hill community can be attributed to the level of civic engagement between the home owners, the public housing residents, and the manager of Cherry Hill Homes. They stood shoulder to shoulder to see that Cherry Hill got its fair share of city services and resources, and in return, they worked to enhance the community's commitment to maximize the opportunity. The Housing Authority wanted to ensure that parents in public housing would have an incentive to exercise control over their children. R. Clarke Davis who succeeded Otho Pinkett as the second manager of Cherry Hill Homes, told the *Afro American* newspaper that to prevent juvenile delinquency from becoming an issue, there was a clause in the public housing leases that made parents responsible for the actions of their children. He said that leases could be revoked if families had children who caused trouble. In an effort to keep children off the streets, the Community Center stayed open until 10 p.m. every night.

Another factor was the management of leisure time with remedial, self-development, and recreational opportunities for the community. From the day that Cherry Hill Homes was dedicated in February 1946, the Community Center building became the focal point for civic and recreational life in Cherry Hill. The art-moderne red brick structure at 2700 Spelman Road was adorned with a bas-relief sculpted panel of a father holding a book interacting with his two children by Henry Berge, a northeast Baltimore sculptor and the son of Edward Berge, the sculptor of several city monuments. The building housed the Cherry Hill Homes rental and maintenance office, the well-baby clinic, meeting rooms, recreation rooms, a kitchen, and a 300-seat auditorium. It even had a TV room where families without TV sets could come and watch TV. The Community Center was designed as a health, education, recreation, and social resource center and meeting place for all the residents of Cherry Hill.

Mrs. Alice Warner Parham, Director of Recreation for Cherry Hill, kept the residents busy with a full schedule of activities for all ages and interests. Mrs. Parham, a native of Mt. Airy, Maryland, was sent to Baltimore in 1916, at the age of 12, to attend Morgan Academy and stayed to attend Morgan State College. While at Morgan, Mrs. Parham became socially engaged as a member of the committee to welcome new students. She also helped to plan activities through the YWCA and was one of the founders of Morgan's Alpha Gamma Chapter of Delta Sigma Theta. After graduating from Morgan State College in 1928, she moved to Youngstown, Ohio, and worked for the YWCA. While there, she met and married her husband, Charles Parham, and moved back to Baltimore and became a central figure in the success of Cherry Hill.

As Cherry Hill Homes celebrated its first anniversary in December 1946, many clubs and organizations had developed around the interests of the community. They included the Cherry Hill Homes Tenant Council whose mission was to hold the tenants and the housing management team accountable for the upkeep of the community; the Cherry Hill Protective Association that was formed by the homeowners when they took the builders to court; the American Veterans Committee and several other veterans groups ; the Ladies Guild; the Mothers Club; the Athletic Association; the Metro Sports Club; the Cherry Hill Bulletin; and the Cub Scouts and Boy Scouts; Republican and Democratic clubs; neighborhood improvement associations, P.T.A.s, youth groups, church clubs and a merchant association.

The Recreation Department sponsored most of the events held at the Community Center including annual Mother-Daughter and Father-Son banquets, weekly youth dances, annual flower shows, and sports banquets. There were weekly classes including academic and homemaking topics that residents could attend to enhance their knowledge and skills. The Recreation Department opened the Cherry Hill swimming pool, at that time a state-of-the-art facility, in 1955. Cherry Hill had first class, award winning athletic teams in all sports. Mrs. Parham made sure that there were no idle minds and hands to be found, all for a nominal fee.

Sidney Rauls Ellis' family moved to Cherry Hill from Fort Holabird, temporary war housing that was later demolished, in 1955. "We moved to the rental townhomes at 611A Bridgeview Road up the street from 159.

My father, Johnnie Rauls worked at Fort Meade, and my mother, Hattie, was a homemaker. My sister and I were the only children at that time. I remember attending the Mother-Daughter Banquet every year. Mommie would get us outfits made just alike, and we wore hats and gloves. There was a musical program with some of the mothers and daughters performing together. Everyone looked so beautiful. Everything about Cherry Hill in those days was done in support of and as a celebration of our strong black families. I also remember how on the last day of school, the priests from St. Veronica would come down to 159 to see our report cards as we were leaving school. They would give us praise for the work we had done and offer encouragement for the next school year. While I was not Catholic, it made me feel good that they would be interested in my academic progress."

James Dow remembers how Mrs. Parham sought out talent for the Community Building's talent shows. "Mrs. Parham started the Toy Band consisting of the young children in the community playing toy instruments. They actually performed before audiences, and those that had an interest graduated to real instruments. Many notable musicians got their start at the Community Building such as Lamont and Ronald Davidson. Ronald played trumpet and Lamont played tenor sax. They both played in many different bands, such as Natural Gas and the Shindells. The Shindells played for many of the Motown groups that came to Baltimore to play at the Royal Theater. Marvin 'Saxman' Hart still performs with bands around the Baltimore area."

Cherry Hill had so many talented early residents that whenever there was a need, someone was able to step up and meet the challenge. Mrs. Myrtle Burge, the resident who spoke at the dedication ceremonies, volunteered her time to teach adults and young people to sew and cook. She held etiquette classes for teenage boys and girls where they learned how to dress, speak, and interact socially. Mrs. Burge belonged to the Ladies Guild of Cherry Hill, and they sponsored cotillions where the young women and men of Cherry Hill were presented and scholarship money raised.

Mr. Shepherd Burge, Jr., Mrs. Burge's husband, had his degree in health and physical education when they came to Baltimore, and he went to work for the Baltimore City Department of Recreation for four years before going to work for the Post Office. Mr. Burge used his recreation experience and contributed 25,000 volunteer hours to benefit the residents of Cherry Hill because Cherry Hill had some of the best sports teams in the city with the trophies to prove it. Mr. Burge also published the *Cherry Hill News*, a monthly newspaper with a circulation throughout Cherry Hill.

It soon became evident that there was a need for the groups to have a working relationship so that they would not duplicate efforts or be working at cross-purposes. That need was filled when the Cherry Hill Co-Ordinating Council was created in late 1947. The greatest achievements of the Council were bringing public transportation to Cherry Hill, defeating an ordinance to put an amusement park in Cherry Hill, keeping the city from building an incinerator next to Cherry Hill, and keeping liquor stores out of Cherry Hill. The first president of the Council was Alexander Brown, who at the time, was also president of the Cherry Hill Protective Association and the United Democratic Club. Mr. Brown was born in Eastman, Georgia, the son of a Baptist minister, and came to Baltimore in 1919 when he was 24. During WWI, he was a senior mechanic in the army and worked for the Federal Government as a mechanic. He moved to Cherry Hill in 1945 when about 25 homes had been built in Cherry Hill Village and along with his wife, Beatrice, raised three daughters.

One of the Council's earliest victories was won in 1947 when it secured a bus route to Cherry Hill. Until that time, residents had to take the bus to Westport and walk to Cherry Hill. In 1948, the Council thwarted the city's effort to place a 16 acre amusement park in Cherry Hill and commercialize a large tract of land. The land was owned by David Pressman (who at that time was a Fairfield grocer but later became a Cherry Hill grocer as well) and was located along Cherry Hill Road between Waterview and Giles Roads. Even though Mr. Pressman repeatedly stated that liquor would not be sold at the park, one of the Council's chief prohibitions, he could not get over the hurdle of the potential for noise and disorderly conduct. The residents of Cherry Hill were not going to have their quality of life disrupted.

The Council organized a petition among the homeowners requiring 20 percent of their signatures to force the City Council to get a three quarters vote to approve the pending ordinance. The tenants of Cherry Hill Homes appealed to Mr. Pinkett to express their opposition to the Housing Authority. The position of all the residents was that Cherry Hill needed a public park for recreation, not a commercial one. With help from the City Plan Commission and the Board of Municipal and Zoning Appeals, the amusement park bill was defeated. The land remained zoned as residential, and Mr. Pressman eventually built private, single-family bungalow style homes along Cherry Hill Road.

Mr. Brown served as president of the Council until 1950 when James L. Bundy, an attorney, was elected. Mr. Bundy was originally from Bluefield, West Virginia, and in 1942, he received a B.S. in secondary education from Bluefield State Teachers College. He moved to Baltimore in June 1942 where he met and married his wife, Sarah Jane Cannon. Mr. Bundy entered the Army Air Force in 1942 and served until 1946. After being discharged from the service, Mr. and Mrs. Bundy purchased a house in Waterview Homes at 601 Cheraton Road. Mr. Bundy was a founding member of the Cherry Hill American Veterans Committee. He entered law school at the University of Maryland and graduated in June 1949. Mr. Bundy worked in the city Law Department where in 1962, he was named an Assistant City Solicitor. In 1974, he was appointed as a District Court Judge.

Like the Burges, Mr. and Mrs. Bundy were Cherry Hill activists. Mrs. Bundy was from Newberry, South Carolina, and was raised in Washington, D.C., where she obtained a diploma in Advanced Nursing from the Freedman's Hospital and was certified as a Civil Defense Officer. Mrs. Bundy also attended the Washington Conservatory and Washington Institute of Music and studied piano in Missouri, Texas, and New York. She did graduate work at the Peabody Conservatory in Baltimore, and was the only black in her class and the first black piano teacher in the Baltimore City school system. Mrs. Bundy served two terms as president of the Council in the mid-1960s.

Early Cherry Hill residents were determined to keep liquor from spoiling the quality of life in their community. The Coordinating Council prides itself with keeping liquor out of Cherry Hill until 1965, however, as quiet as it's kept, a liquor license was granted for the tavern that was turned into the rectory for Saint Veronica's first pastor, Father Robbins. That license was granted to Dorothy Castranda in July 1944. According to the Breinhan history, Mrs. Castranda's husband, John, had an automobile junkyard on some of the property eventually sold to the Archdiocese for St. Veronica's Church and Jerome Kahn, the developer of Waterview Homes.

John Nelson remembers the tavern and remembers that the tavern was for whites only, and his mother prohibited him from playing near the tavern. The tavern closed when the church purchased it in 1951. When the Cherry Hill Shopping Center was built, the drugstore, Segal's Pharmacy, tried to obtain a license for a package good store next door to it, and was turned down because of the lobbying efforts of the Council. Other early presidents of the Council included Walter Baker, Gladys Tyler, William Murphy, Reverend Edgar Ward, and John Hawkins, and they were all of one accord—keep liquor stores out of Cherry Hill. The Council was successful in this endeavor until 1965.

On July 29, 1965, the liquor Board denied a license to Leah Molofsky to put a liquor store in the shopping center. She submitted a petition with 650 signatures supporting her request that stated the liquor store was necessary for the public convenience and in the public interest. Her representatives argued that because residents often bootlegged liquor from their homes or automobiles at premium prices, a liquor store was also necessary for public safety. The Council argued that the license should not be granted because the community qualified for anti-poverty aid with more than 60 percent of residents earning less than $3,000 annually. The School Board objected to the liquor store arguing that it would be located less than 300 feet from school 160, and that 75 per cent of the community's 28,000 residents were minors. The Liquor Board denied Ms. Molofsky's application for the license.

Ms. Molofsky appealed the denial, and on November 15, 1965, Judge James K. Cullen reversed the decision and directed that a package goods beer, wine and liquor license be issued to Ms. Molofsky's store. The Judge stated that nearly every shopping center in the city had a liquor store, and it was an inconvenience to the residents of Cherry Hill not to have one. The Liquor Board had argued in its opinion that the license was not required for public convenience and accommodation, and that granting a license would unduly disturb the peace of the residents. However, Judge Cullen noted that the last refusal to the area was in 1949, and that since that time, the area had grown and the residents were entitled to have a liquor store. Ironically, Ms. Molofsky's attorney was Milton B. Allen, a black attorney who was a champion to black Baltimoreans, and who later became the Baltimore City State's Attorney.

10.

Cherry Hill Commerce

When John moved to Cherry Hill in 1944, there was no shopping center. He said that many of the families in Cherry Hill Village shopped in the Glen Burnie area. John said that there was a small grocery store they could walk to on Hanover Street called The Fruit Stand. At the time that Cherry Hill Homes were being dedicated in February 1946, the Cherry Hill Shopping Center was in the midst of construction. Families who moved to Cherry Hill from other parts of the city shopped at the facilities they were familiar with before they moved to Cherry Hill. Baltimore had its fair share of corner grocery stores and open-air markets to meet its citizens' food demands. Cherry Hill was close to downtown Baltimore, Lexington Market, Cross Street Market, and Hollins Market. Others migrating from West Baltimore patronized Lafayette Market.

In the mid-to-late 1940s thru the early 1960s, many food products and services were obtained through home delivery. The Cloverland and Greenspring dairies delivered dairy products to Cherry Hill. Those were the days of glass milk bottles with notes left in them with delivery instructions for the milkman. We had bread deliveries from Rice's bakery. Archer's Laundry came to Cherry Hill to pick up and deliver laundry and dry cleaning. Don't forget the Jack and Jill and Good Humor Ice Cream men. In spite of the fact that our center of commerce did not open until mid-1946, Cherry Hill residents managed to obtain their retail commodities and services.

Cherry Hill was also serviced by Jacob W. Logan, a young black entre-preneur, and his grocery bus. Mr. Logan, better known to Cherry Hill children as Daddy Logan, was at one time a Cherry Hill resident. He saw the potential for mobile food service in the community, and he initially outfitted a truck with groceries and drove through the neighborhoods selling his wares. He then came to the realization that a school bus would be more accessible, so he transitioned his merchandise to school busses that travelled through various south Baltimore communities as a mobile grocery store. Daddy Logan also had a grocery store at 101 W. Hamburg Street operated by his wife, Estelle. He even had his own brand of bread, Daddy Logan's Bread, which was baked in Crisfield, Maryland.

Daddy Logan was born in Jenkins, Kentucky, on June 28, 1920. He remembers, "My family moved to Marion, North Carolina, during the Depression. I left home at 12 years old and went to work for 3 different white families in North Carolina. I left North Carolina when I was 18 and went to work for a white family in Scarsdale, NY. I helped to take care of the family's children, and I learned to caddy for the husband of the family. When I asked to learn to play golf, my employer told me that black people did not have the ability to learn to play golf. I picked up what I could before I left the family's employ." When Daddy Logan left Scarsdale, it was to go to Fort Bragg for induction into the service for the war. According to Daddy Logan, he told the induction staff that he didn't like water, and he didn't like to fly, and they did not take him into the service. He left Ft. Bragg and came to Baltimore where he got a job working in the defense industry at the Sparrows Point Shipyard where after saving enough money, he was able to purchase his first grocery truck.

Shopping on Daddy Logan's bus was a thrilling experience. He had all the penny candy a child could want, and typically, the children drove his business. They would see the bus in the area and run in to ask their moms for money to spend for candy. Then the mothers would come out to shop on the bus or send the children with a note and money for the items they wanted. If a mother couldn't pay that day, he would let her have the items until she could pay. His business was so profitable, that he was able to buy a house in Glen Burnie. In spite of being told that he could not learn golf, Daddy Logan learned to play golf at the age of 73. Up until his death on November 23, 2017, Thanksgiving Day, he sponsored Daddy Logan's Golf Challenge to get other seniors out on the golf course.

When the shopping center finally opened, it was a showcase of all the goods and services available in any shopping center of its time—except for a liquor store. There was an A&P supermarket, a drug store, a men's clothing shop, a barber shop, beauty shop, a dry cleaners, pool hall, a hardware store, the Hill movie theater, a beauty shop, a carry out shop, and a women's and children's clothing store.

The shopping center was built by Harry Myerberg, whose brothers had built Cherry Hill Village. The Myerberg family was an old-line Baltimore real estate family headed by Nathan J. Myerberg, a Polish immigrant, who founded N. J. Myerberg and Sons. Michael M. Myerberg, one of Nathan's five sons, was a theatrical impresario who once owned the Brooks Atkinson Theater on Broadway. Harry followed Michael to New York and dabbled in the entertainment industry, managing Warner Brothers Theaters in New York and northern New Jersey before returning to Baltimore and the family real estate business.

The Myerberg Brothers, as the company came to be called after Nathan's death, left a prolific imprint all over Baltimore and the surrounding area. During WWII, Myerberg Brothers built military housing at Fort Meade, about 10 miles from Cherry Hill. When the war was over, Harry met with Eleanor Roosevelt to discuss strategies for desegregating the construction sites. Nancy Myerberg Dirkin, one of Harry Meyerberg's two daughters, and Executive Vice President for Policy of The Leadership Conference on Civil and Human Rights, told me, "My father believed in the dignity of all people, and that everyone deserved to live in decent housing. He was a civil rights advocate all of his life. He was instrumental in bringing Marian Anderson to sing at the Lyric Theater after she was denied the right to sing at Constitution Hall." Although Nancy was young when Cherry Hill was built, she said she remembers that life in Baltimore was a very segregated situation.

Mr. Myerberg worked with the Cherry Hill Community even after the shopping center was constructed. Whenever there was a need for space, he was approached to provide it. When the churches were being built, he rented out vacant stores to accommodate worship services. When Hemingway Temple's tent burned down, he offered them a vacant store for services. He permitted the schools to use the Hill Theater for their programs. There has always been a strong bond and working relationship between Baltimore's black and Jewish communities.

Betty's mother, Beulah Pinkney, used to work at the Peggy Ruth Shoppe, the women's and children's store. "The Peggy Ruth Shoppe was owned and operated by Julius and Margaret Nathanson. My mom began working there as a sales person, and as time passed, we all became like family. The whole Shopping center was like another community. Soon, another grocery store opened, Pressman Brothers, and when they outgrew their building, they built a grocery store and another pharmacy across the street from the original shopping center. As time went on, the Nathansons decided to sell the store, and while the store was being remodeled for the new owner, Mrs. Pinkney went to work across the street at Pressman Brothers Drug Store. When the new owner of the dress store, Jerry Sidle, opened Sidle's of Cherry Hill (his father owned Sidle's in Glen Burnie), he asked Mrs. Pinkney to come back to work in the dress shop. In the late 1960s, Sidle wanted to open a new store in the newly constructed Harundale Mall in Glen Burnie, and he convinced Mrs. Pinkney that she had the ability to run her own business and sold the store to her. In 1968, Mrs. Pinkney opened Michele's, Your Gateway to Fashion.

Christine Middleton Bazemore lived at 614 Cheraton Road behind the shopping center. She and her family moved there because their house in Fairfield had burned down. Since her father had relatives already living in Cherry Hill, he moved his family there in 1957. Christine says, "My Aunt, Anna Davis, owned the beauty shop in the shopping center. I remember stopping in to her shop to get my hair done during the week and on Saturdays on my way to the movies. The ladies would be talking and reading magazines, but they would always seem to be glad to see me. Aunt Anna taught me about making goals and sticking to them, and I did just that. I attended the Community College of Baltimore and went on to the University of Baltimore where I got my degree in sociology." Christine believes that living in Cherry Hill and being exposed to the strong work and entrepreneurial ethic made her the no nonsense person that she is today. It made her realize that you could be whatever you wanted to be regardless of where you lived.

The opening of the shopping center meant employment opportunities for Cherry Hill residents. In those days, the hardware store was more like a variety store because it carried household goods as well as small appliances. Linda Bowman's father worked part-time at the hardware store in the back room repair shop. "He could repair anything electrical from TVs to toasters," said Linda.

Thomas Weaver, a resident of Dupont Manor on Woodview Road, worked at the A&P right out of high school in 1966. Thomas remembers, "I was working for the A&P when affirmative action in employment came along. I worked in the produce department, when one day my manager came to me and said he was going to train me to be a manager. He said, 'It's pretty much what you do now except with some bull shit paper work.' I stayed with A&P, though not with the Cherry Hill store, until I retired as a produce manager."

Rethia shared that her first job was at Segal's Drug Store. "I started working at Segal's in my senior year in high school. When I went off to college, I would come back and work on my breaks. Segal's had a sit down fountain and lunch counter, pharmacy and up front counter cash register. I remember being very embarrassed when men bought condoms and when women bought Lydia Pinkham pills. Both items were kept behind the counter. Older men would ask for the pharmacist, but of course there were some men that seemed to enjoy my embarrassment. Still I am grateful that I was able to get a job in the community."

Joan Ellis Gaither got her first job at Segal's when she was 16. "I worked the cash register for the lunch counter. I felt so independent having a job and getting a pay check. I remember that I got my hair done with my first paycheck and was planning to go to a party. However, I had not asked my mom. I went home with my cute hairstyle and hormones pumping and *told* my mom I was going to the party. My mom told me no, I was not going to any party. My mom went to grab me for talking back to her, but I ran out of the house before she could get to me. I am one of seven children, and all my mom had to do was to send them out to find me. When they finally did and brought me home, my mom was waiting for me—with a water pistol. She had me sit down, and she came up to me with the water pistol and quoted back to me everything I had said to her punctuated with a squirt from the water gun for every curl in my hairdo. That day I learned a very important lesson—don't talk back to mom."

Wes remembers Saturdays at the Hill Theater where the box office had a red line on the window. If your height was under the line, you paid the children's admission price. If you were taller than the line or 12-years-old, you paid the adult admission. This could be the difference in whether you had enough to buy that box of Jujy Fruits. Wesley said, "We would bend our knees as we approached the pay window. We had to memorize a different birthdate to pretend we were younger than we were. Once past the box office attendant and inside the theater, we had to get past the ticket taker who would ask, 'When we were born?' If we stumbled reciting the date, or otherwise gave up the truth, we had to get out of line and turn around and embarrassingly walk past those in line back to the ticket window to pay full price. Or, if we were lucky, one of the guys in our group who managed to get past the ticket taker would go down the aisle to the exit and open the side door for three or four of us to sneak in. We would spend all day Saturday—usually from noon until 5 p.m. watching 3 first run movies and a cartoon. When we got bored, we would run around the movie throwing popcorn on the other kids who retaliated in kind when you least expected it."

According to Betty, "Going to the movies on Saturday was a regular event. With six children in the family there was not a lot of money. When my parents didn't have enough money to send the three older children, my brother Joe would figure out ways to be sure that we would all be able to go. If he didn't have enough money from his *Afro* paper route, he would get the money by selling comic books or other means. I remember one of his more successful ventures. He would fill my mother's big wash tub with water, put it out in front of the house, place some of Momma's saucers on top of the water, and then tell the other kids to toss pennies to land on the saucers. If they landed, he had any number of neat toys that he would give as prizes. Once he had collected enough money, he would close up shop and we would all head out for our weekly venture at the movies.

"The Hill Theater was not just a movie house. It served other purposes. I remember 'The Young Folks Theater.' We would go upstairs in the theater and participate in drama and in tap dance. This was quite an experience for us and I recall thinking that someday they might be seeing me on stage or on screen. The theater was also used as a site for worship. In the early days, we had no church building in which to worship. Before St. Veronica Church was constructed, we worshipped at the community building, the hardware store, and, believe it or not, the Hill Theater."

The Cherry Hill Shopping Center was the center of town, and anytime a politician or famous person came to Cherry Hill, this is where they stopped. This was the site for beauty pageants and the Grand Stand for parades. It became a site for boxing legends when in July 1968, Muhammad Ali, the former heavyweight boxing champion, stopped by to spar and joke around with a crowd of adults and teenagers. He was in town to speak at Mosque No. 6 of the Nation of Islam on Wilson Street the next day. According to the *Sun*, he shadow boxed all over the parking lot and exchanged jabs with the teenage boys. Women offered him their babies to be kissed. What a memorable way to pass a hot summer day.

11.

Law And Order

Long before the construction of Cherry Hill Homes, Cherry Hill had a dubious relationship with the police. In the late 19th and early 20th centuries, the area was well known for its nefarious characters and hang outs. Tales of secret play areas and youth gangs having Huckleberry Finn-like adventures circulated widely. The area is said to have housed two disreputable "resorts for the colored," Razor Park and Lincoln Park. There was a Fish House and a place called Kelly's Park that would have occasional fish fries, barbecues, and bull roasts and draw what were reported to be loud, rowdy, colored crowds. Police were often called to the area to maintain order.

Black organizations and clubs would frequent the area, and sometimes black churches would hold baptisms in the Patapsco River. The August 27, 1901, *Sun* reported on the eleventh annual celebration of the Colored Citizens League, which was held the day before, noting that 3,500 people attended the celebration eating 100 barrels of fried fish and 500 loaves of bread used for fish sandwiches. Professor Frank Johnson's Band Furnished dance music and there were sermons by several ministers. There was an endorsement of the *Sun* for its fairness to the colored race, and Booker T. Washington sent a letter containing his regrets at not being able to attend. Cherry Hill was a known quantity at the turn of the century, and at that time was part of Baltimore County. It wasn't until 1918 that Cherry Hill was annexed to Baltimore City. When Cherry Hill became a part of Baltimore City, it became the responsibility of the Southern Police District.

According to Leonard, "The Southern District was created in 1845 and was located first at Montgomery and Sharp streets. It moved to Ostend and Patapsco Streets in 1896, staying at that location until the district moved to 10 Cherry Hill Road in the Cherry Hill community in 1986 where it remains to this day. At the time the district moved into Cherry Hill, it was viewed as a positive anchor institution.

"The Baltimore City Police Department was integrated in 1937 when it hired the first black police officer, a woman, Officer Violet Hill Whyte. She was assigned and worked out of the Western District for 30 years. In 1938, the Department hired its first black male officers. They were assigned to plain clothes because a uniform was a sign of authority to the community, and the Department did not want for these officers to be seen as authority figures. The first black male officers hired were Walter T. Eubanks, Harry S. Scott, Milton Gardner, and J. Hiram Butler Jr."

Leonard goes on to say, "The Department was not fully integrated until 1966 when black officers were permitted to ride in patrol cars. Prior to 1966, black officers were limited to foot patrol. These officers were quarantined in rank, barred from patrolling white neighborhoods and would often only be given specialty assignments in positions in the Narcotics Division or as under cover plain clothes officers. They were not allowed to be seated at daily roll call, but had to stand in the back of the room while the white officers sat. Being treated badly by their own kind, it is easy to see why in their frustration, they would abuse less powerful people—the black community."

Leonard said, "In Cherry Hill we knew, by officers' actions, that they were conducting themselves as an occupying army—not the guardians of the community they should have been. This department was slow to change technologically, socially, professionally, and in a sense of fundamental fairness. Growing up in Cherry Hill, we knew to stay away from police officers. Policing the community became the responsibility of the adults who lived in the community. The crime rate in Cherry Hill appeared to be very low at the time with minor misdemeanor crime taking up the bulk of officers' time.

"Many black police officers were assigned to Cherry Hill over the years. However, they did not treat the citizens in the community any better than their white counterparts. Officers were visible, spending most of their time in the shopping center, sitting in police vehicles, flirting with the women of the community. They were by no means guardians to the community with the mandate to help citizens solve problems. Police were stationed to suppress crime and seemingly personal liberty. On the occasions police were called for service (the nature of the original call didn't matter) someone was either brutally arrested or brutally beaten. Growing up, we did not consider police our friend. In fact, we kept our distance from them."

According to a May 7, 1949, *Sun* editorial from Mrs. Murphy, in her capacity as President of the Cherry Hill Mothers' Club, policing in Cherry Hill consisted of two police call boxes and a patrol car which made regular rounds. The editorial was written in response to a police officer being shot behind Cherry Hill School #159 and asked for more police protection for the area. Mrs. Murphy made the point that if the young man who shot the officer admitted to doing so to "scare him," Cherry Hill needed more attention from the Police Department because of the on-going construction conditions in the development. There were still wooded areas through which residents had to pass to go to school, church, and the shopping center. The street lighting needed improvement and streets were still being paved.

Mrs. Murphy wrote, "We, in Cherry Hill, have been clamoring for better police protection ever since this community was started. It is too bad, but perhaps now that a policeman has been shot, we will get results. Perhaps now we will have foot patrolmen, and colored ones at that."

The Cherry Hill community did have one champion on the police force. He was Officer Oliver Murdock. Leonard remembers, "Officer Murdock had a military bearing. He was tall, broad shouldered, athletic, in great physical condition, and well read. He was clean shaven, his uniform was always sharp and crisp. Officer Murdock spoke perfect English, all the time. He never used slang or the popular colloquialisms of the day. We were referred to as 'young men' or 'gentlemen'. Officer Murdock was the guardian the community needed. He was a role model and a protector, but he held us accountable for our actions. Years later, when I joined the force, I had the perfect role model."

Leonard said, "I had two encounters with the police in Cherry Hill. In the ninth grade a schoolmate and I were walking to school one morning from Bethune Road. We were late for school, but on our way, books and lunch in hand. At the shopping center a white officer stopped us and questioned us. He decided he would take us to school. He dropped us off at the front door. It felt like every window in that school building had a face at it. The entire situation was embarrassing and demeaning. I don't think the officer meant to be helpful because Cherry Hill Junior High School was within walking distance from where he picked us up."

Leonard recalls another incident. "A year later, I was in the tenth grade attending Baltimore City College in northeast Baltimore. One

Linda G. Morris

Wednesday evening at about 6:00 p.m., two friends and I walked to the shopping center from Round Road. I went into the dry cleaners to retrieve an article of clothing. My two friends waited outside the store. I completed my business, walked outside the store and observed my friends against the wall under arrest. The white arresting officer asked if I was with the two, I said I was, and he placed me under arrest also. We asked, but were never told why we were being arrested. We were taken to the Southern District lockup and charged with obstructing pedestrian passage on the public street (sidewalk) and disorderly conduct.

"All of our mothers came down to the station at separate times to get their sons out of jail, but each mother reasoned that it would not be right to take one son and leave the other two in jail. The mothers knew each other, and they knew all of us. They decided that since court was the next morning, we should all spend the night in jail together. Of course we three did not agree with their reasoning. My father worked the 4 p.m. to midnight shift and wasn't available at that time, but I am sure he would not have made that decision. He came to court the next morning on behalf of all of us and got us released because of his testimony to the judge.

"We were all juveniles, no criminal record, and all of us were enrolled at Baltimore City College, one of the top high schools in the city located in northeast Baltimore. The officer testified in court under oath why he arrested us. His testimony was all false fabrication which the judge saw right through. When the officer completed his testimony, the judge dismissed the case without hearing from us and directed us to go to school."

Other officers who lived in Cherry Hill and joined the police force include Lt. Melvin Freeman, Spelman Road; Police Commissioner (ret.) Edward Woods, Denham Circle; Det. Marcellus Ward, Seagull Avenue; Officer Leak Van Landingham, Bethune Road; Officer Willie Purdue, Cheraton Road; and Officer William Pitt, Cheraton Road.

Houston Murphy remembers getting into trouble stealing a neighbor's grapes. "One day in August 1961 as I completed the weeding of my mother's flower garden, my friend Steven explained to me that the grapes were ripe and nobody was home at Mr. Mickle's trailer. He sketched out his plan of how we would sneak to the grape vines by going through the alley behind Mr. Mickle's trailer, using our 'Indian crawl' under his fence so as not to be seen. We assembled our crew, which consisted of Michael Holland, Michal Manigo and Fern and executed our plan. We were filling our brown paper bags with our stolen grapes when suddenly Mr. Mickle arrived home and chased us off. He was hollering, 'I saw you and know who you are, Houston Murphy!'

"I was immediately scared. We ran to Steven's house on Cherryland Road. Steven's mother was at work, and we gorged ourselves on our stolen grapes, laughing and congratulating ourselves on our close call with Mr. Mickle and the clean get-away. It plagued me that Mr. Mickle had recognized me to the point where he called me by name. I knew it was simply a matter of time before he called my parents who would dole out my inevitable punishment.

"All of a sudden, there was a loud banging on Steven's door. We all got really quiet. Steven looked out the window, but all he saw was a police car with its single dome light flashing. In a loud, booming voice, we heard, 'This is the POLICE! Open the door RIGHT NOW, or I'll bust the door down!' I walked down the stairs and opened the door. Standing in front of me was this burley, fierce, imposing, black policeman who barked, 'Where are the rest of your friends who stole the grapes?' It was Officer Murdock."

Officer Murdock let most of the other boys go while he put Houston and his friend Steven, who were about ten years old at the time, in hand cuffs. The cuffs kept slipping off of their wrists, so he cuffed them together above the elbow. Officer Murdock put them is his squad car and drove the boys out of Cherry Hill, across the Hanover Street Bridge to the Southern District Police Station where the boys were placed in a cell. He allowed them to place a phone call, and Houston called his father.

Houston said, "I burst out crying uncontrollably before I was even able to tell my father what had happened. He kept saying over the phone, 'Calm down, Houston, and tell me where you are.' Through my tears, I told him I was in jail. He said, 'OK, I'll be right there', and hung up. What seemed like hours later, Officer Murdock brought Steven and me into the interview room where my father, Steven's mother, Mrs. Lewis, and Mr. Mickle were waiting. They stood, and my father asked Officer Murdock, very formally, 'What are the charges?' Officer Murdock said in his deep baritone voice, 'Destruction of property, grand theft, and breaking and entering.' It seemed like an hour before the adults turned to me and Steven, and my father said that Officer Murdock would be releasing us to our parents' custody."

Houston had not noticed at first, but Mr. Mickle had brought a switch with him. As the victim, he was allowed to spank both of the culprits as punishment. He pulled up a chair, told both boys to drop their pants, and took them over his knee and whipped them, first Houston and then Steven.

Much later, the boys found out that this was a grand conspiracy by all adult parties involved to scare them straight. Houston also found out that his father and other Cherry Hill lawyers, and law enforcement personnel played out this drama countless times throughout Cherry Hill scaring kids straight trying to discourage them from a life of crime.

12.

Coming of Age

We led idyllic lives growing up in Cherry Hill. The structures of family, community, education, and religion shaped us into a very well socialized and confident generation ready to take on the world—or so we thought. Growing up in a segregated, self-sufficient black community had given us a false sense of security that the world functioned with the same core values that we had learned growing up in Cherry Hill—love your neighbor, work hard, and respect everyone. We weren't ready for the punch to the gut the world had waiting for us when we left for our first socialization experience outside of our homogeneous cocoon. Although we were often reminded we were black in isolated situations with our parents, as children on our own, we had no idea of the hurtfulness and systemic nature of racism.

My introduction to being treated differently was when I was perhaps four and being taken to the restroom in the Julius Gutman Department Store in downtown Baltimore. I was just learning to read and to sound out words. I noticed that there were two doors, and I began reading aloud and pointing at the signs—"White Ladies" and "Colored Women"—trying to pronounce the syllables and asking my mother what they meant. I could tell by the way my mother shushed me and pulled me by the arm through the crowd of women passing through both doors, that this was not the time and place for a reading lesson or discussion on segregation.

Looking back, I can see how my parents shielded me and my siblings from the ugliness of Jim Crow and segregation. It really became evident once we got a car and started venturing out on road trips. I remember one

Saturday, my dad was going to take us for a ride, but he wanted to get seat covers put on our 1949 green Plymouth (which he bought in 1956) before we left. He packed us in the car early and drove us to Rayco, a company that sold and installed seat covers in Glen Burnie, thinking that it would take maybe an hour, and we could be on our way. We waited there half the day, while we watched other cars come and go, but we never got waited on. My Dad decided to leave and take us back home. It was only in later years that I learned why we spent all that time to no avail. I can only imagine how it made my Dad feel as a man. I'm sure it had to make him angry, but if it did, he never showed it to me and my siblings.

Then there was the time we went out for a Sunday drive up to Thurmont, Maryland, to visit a snake farm, and our car broke down. My brother, John, was fascinated by these creepy crawlers, and whenever we showed an interest in something, my parents tried to expand our experience with it usually with a road trip. My mom and I shared a fear of snakes, so we stayed in the car, along with Judy, while John and my dad went in. Our Plymouth broke down on the way back home. Whenever the car broke down, my father went under the hood and could usually get us running. By the time he got us back on the road, we were hungry. This was before the days of fast food outlets dotting the landscape, so my dad stopped at a lunch room while we all stayed in the car. He came back out, with no food and silently drove off. When my mother asked him what happened, he said the owner told him to drive to the back of the lunch room and he would take his order. Needless to say, we drove the two hours or so back to Cherry Hill hungry.

For Houston, car trips brought the lesson home to him too. "We took regular road trips to various destinations where my father and mother would carefully map out our routes so as to avoid places that discriminated against Black people. We always avoided the Double T Diner on Route 40. On long trips, my parents always consulted the Green Book." The Negro Motorist Green Book, as it was formally titled, was a book published by Victor Green, a New York City mailman, who sought to keep black drivers out of harm's way and to save them the embarrassment of attempting to patronize segregated establishments. Once the Civil Rights Act of 1964 was passed outlawing segregation in public accommodations, the book, which was updated annually, became obsolete. With the current state of affairs across the country, there is talk of reviving the publication.

Yvette said her awakening came in downtown Baltimore. "I was seven, and my sisters were six and four. My mother took us to buy winter coats during an after-the-season 50% off sale at Stewart's Department store downtown. The saleswoman told Mom there was no dressing room for Negroes, so we would have to leave. Mom began trying coats on us in the aisles. By the time the woman came back with her supervisor, my mother had chosen the coats, and was ready with the cash to pay for them. I remember feeling for the first time there was something wrong with my 'blackness'. We talked about it when we got home, and I learned there were places I could not go just because I was black. I remember feeling angry about the unfairness of it."

Joan shared her experience going with her grandmother to purchase a hat when she was nine-years-old. Joan said, "The women in my family have always worn hats. My grandmother loved hats and one day, she took me with her downtown to Stewart's Department Store to buy one. My grandmother selected the hat that she wanted and handed it to the sales woman. I piped up and asked the sales woman, 'Can't she try it on?' The sales woman replied, "No." Joan came back with a very logical retort, "What if it doesn't fit?" The sales woman said, "No self-respecting white woman would want that hat after a nigger had it on." Joan said, "All I could do was look at the lady in disbelief because my nine-year-old mind could not comprehend how my grandmother trying on a hat could be so detrimental to a white woman."

When you are a child who has been shielded from the ugliness of segregation, you just can't comprehend why people are treating you the way they do. You approach situations thinking that people are going to deal with you in good faith. When they don't, you think it's something wrong with them—not you. It's a bitter lesson that you learn sooner or later, and when you learn it, you know you are growing up.

Calvin's introduction came when he was in the second grade in 1954. "I saw on TV how the students who integrated Southern High School had to walk through angry crowds of whites with a police escort just to go to school. Some of those students were from Cherry Hill. It was a frightening scene for me as a seven-year-old."

Wesley shares his worst memory of Cherry Hill. "On a hot summer day in August, a group of us guys, five to seven of us, were out walking in the woods, exploring the area across the train tracks. We came upon an enclave of really nicely built single family homes. Apparently some of the residents of the homes saw us, and perceived us to be a threat. Unbeknownst to us, when we got back across the tracks, we turned and saw a group of white men with long barrel rifles pointing at us from across the other side of the tracks. They were screaming something like, 'You stay away from here.' We never really understood what or why they were yelling at us. Yet, we got the message. We continued our walks in the woods, but we made sure to stay away from the white folks homes. The scene of those white men armed and screaming at us in a threatening manner is an image of Baltimore whites that is forever etched in my mind."

Wesley recalls a downtown segregation experience. One day when he was coming home after football practice at Forest Park High School in northwest Baltimore, Wesley missed his usual bus to Cherry Hill which he caught near the White Castle coffee shop. He decided to go in to get a donut, but the waitress waited on other customers—never acknowledging him. While waiting, he would step outside to see if his bus was coming. When he stepped back in after what seemed like a long time being over-looked, Wesley asked the waitress, "Can I get a donut?" To his surprise she replied, "We don't serve your kind here."

Wesley said, "Her statement shocked me. I looked around at the faces of the people in the shop and knew that I was in the wrong place. I had a strong urge to pick up the big metal trash can that was at the end of the counter and throw it through the window when I saw my bus pulling up to the corner stop. I made the choice to not act and vandalize the store—but to get on the bus. My life, no doubt, would have changed had I reacted to the racism I experienced that day."

Growing up in Cherry Hill, knowing the beauty of nature and being part of a loving community, we had sense enough to know that this behav-ior and those who practiced it had to be outside of the norm. There was something wrong with them—not us. It did not phase us because we were raised in Cherry Hill (R.I.C.H.) [an acronym copyrighted by Michael Bat-tle, a current Cherry Hill resident, for use on active wear]. To have been raised in Cherry Hill in the early days with black people who lived their lives in pursuit of the elusive American dream was to be rich in a soulful existence.

Yvette remembers, "In middle school, came great changes. Some of us stayed and attended Cherry Hill Junior High #180, but many of us left our neighborhood to attend junior high at Garrison, Lemmel, and Ben Franklin. We learned to navigate the city on transit buses. Girls went to Light Street or Lexington Street with their moms to buy their first nylon stockings, and training bras—a great day indeed. I remember getting my first pair of cha-cha heels at Easter when I was in sixth grade. In seventh grade, I began babysitting for neighbors' kids. I had a single mom, and five siblings, so earning my own money was a very big deal. I could save it or spend it as I wished and felt very grown up. I would make weekly trips to the hardware store to buy the latest top 40 hit records, 45's. By the time I was in in the ninth grade, I had quite a record collection, and our house was the house for dancing in stocking feet on Friday and Saturday evenings. My mom wanted to know where I was and who I was with, so it was just easier to invite groups of friends to my house.

"I went to Western High School downtown at Howard and Center Streets. I got a work permit when I was 14 years old, and my first after school job was as a recreation aide at the recreation center in the community building. It was there I first knew I wanted to teach young children. In 10th grade I was allowed to go on my first real date. His name was Kenny, and he lived in the same courtyard as my cousin Beverly in the projects in East Baltimore. He had met my mom on several of our visits to Beverly's. On a Saturday afternoon, he came to Cherry Hill on the transit bus, picked me up, and we rode the #15 bus to the Harlem movie on Edmondson and Gilmor Street. He paid my way into the theater, and bought me a hotdog and a drink. I felt really special, since it cost him a week's allowance to do it.

"In 11th grade I got my first semiformal dress, pale yellow chiffon, and real high heels. It was for junior prom. My date was Barry Curtis, who was in my class throughout elementary school, and I had known since kindergarten. We took a taxi to the Algonquin Hotel on Cathedral Street, walked down Park Avenue to the White Rice Inn for Chinese food afterward, then took a taxi home. I paid for dinner, and Barry paid for the taxis. We had a ball.

"Young people from Cherry Hill ventured out of Cherry Hill to roller skate at the Coliseum on Monroe Street or to go bowling at the Lafayette Bowling Alley on Lafayette Avenue and Bentalou Street. These were favorite hangouts for Cherry Hill teens on Friday and Saturday evenings. Yvette said, "In the winter, we looked forward to snow days when schools were cancelled, because everybody was outside until the wee hours of the morning sliding down the hills on Spelman Road, Round Road, Denham Circle, the hill behind the community building, the one behind #159 and #163 elementary schools. Clay Hill on Cherry Hill Road was dangerous, but great fun because it was so steep. If you weren't very careful, you could shoot right off the hill into traffic. That did not stop us kids at all. We were all out there, hundreds of us on sleds, trashcan tops, washing machine tops, cardboard boxes, and whatever we could find. I don't remember feeling afraid, or unsafe. It was always great fun. We would return home cold, soaking wet, but happy.

"It wasn't until I was in college that I realized what a great childhood I had growing up in Cherry Hill. By then I had made friends who lived all over the city, who had vastly different growing up experiences, and were influenced as I was, by the neighborhood they grew up in. Some of my friends were from the east side. They lived in row homes or in high rise projects on paved streets with very little green spaces in which to play. They had to go to Clifton Park, Druid Hill Park, or Chick Webb Rec Center to find enough room to get a baseball game going. Otherwise, they played in the streets and alleys, or on vacant lots in their neighborhoods.

"Some of my friends were from the west side, where their parents were home owners, and they had more material things than we did in Cherry Hill. Many of them lived on tree lined streets with manicured front lawns and fenced back yards. Lots of them had cars in their families, and could get to where they needed to be without riding for hours on the transit buses. Some of my friends lived in midtown (McCullough Street, Druid Hill Avenue, Pennsylvania Avenue). Many of their parents were home owners as well. They also lived with paved streets and sidewalks and very little green space. They could go to Lafayette Square, Harlem Park, or Druid Hill Park to play. Otherwise, they too played in the streets or alleys nearby. Even though I may not have had as much materially as they, I had so much more."

Frances attended the August 28, 1963, March on Washington for Jobs and Freedom. She said, "As an anxious 17 year old rising Eastern High School senior, I boarded the bus in the Cherry Hill Shopping Center going to the March on Washington for Jobs and Freedom. I and perhaps many others, had no idea how historic this March would become. My Aunt, Mrs. Cora Matthews Glenn, funded my trip. She worked for the National Security Agency in Ft. Meade, Maryland, and the agency had restricted leave for August 28, 1963.

"The atmosphere on the bus was one of excitement as well as confidence that things would be peaceful. Until I was in the midst of the crowds in DC, I could not have ever imagined being in an enormous mass of an estimated 250,000 people sharing their joy, spirit, songs, and positive outlook. The March is regarded as one the largest demonstrations ever seen in the nation's capital, and one of the first to have extensive television coverage.

"The military policemen were well armed, but even they were smiling. At no time did I feel afraid. I didn't know that my future husband was somewhere in the masses with a group from the Bronx, and I wouldn't meet him until 1965. Leaving the March to return home, my feelings were that changes were coming because we clearly demonstrated that we could 'get along.' Fortunately, progress has been made, but unfortunately, somethings have remained the same."

Betty married in 1964. "I married Leslie Harris who lived on Terra Firma Road. I knew him for quite a while as he attended schools #160 and #180. Although we had known each other for a long time, we did not begin dating until after we matriculated at Morgan State College. We began traveling back and forth together and eventually began dating. He was an art major there and I majored in Spanish. We married and moved into the newly constructed Cherrydale Apartments where we lived with our first two children. I had no desire to live any other place. When my mother-in-law moved from her home on Terra Firma Road, she suggested that we rent her house. We moved there, and we had our third son. We stayed until 1978.

"I can recall the riots of 1968 after Dr. Martin Luther King was assassinated. I was teaching at Northwestern High School on Park Heights Avenue. For several days the city was shut down because of rioting. We had no rioting in Cherry Hill. We were peaceful there. The proprietors were our friends, and I don't think it entered anyone's mind to destroy the businesses that served them. Once things opened back up, I was shocked at the destruction that I saw as I drove up Park Heights Avenue. It was no longer the fashionable area that I remembered driving up just a week before. But Cherry Hill had not changed."

When asked what person in Cherry Hill, other than a family member, inspired you the most, the names E. Valeria and Madeline Murphy, no relation, came up most often from the women on this project. As the Director of Religious Education for the Presbyterian Church, E. Valeria Murphy was responsible for the Sunday School program and the Vacation Bible School. Mrs. Madeline Murphy was the Director of Community Services. She started the day care and breakfast program at the church which lead to a full array of social services programs. Together they touched many of the lives of the first generation and influenced them into their adulthood.

"As a young adult, I was influenced most by Mrs. Madeline Murphy," said Darlene McClain-Smith. "She is the reason I am a community activist today. Mrs. Murphy recruited me to work on her campaign when she decided to run for City Council. As a result, I became overwhelmingly fascinated by the political process that focused on change and making things better for our community. After working on her campaign, I decided to attend Coppin State College as a non-traditional student, the single mother of two children, seeking a degree in Political Science. I graduated Cum Laude with a bachelor's degree with a major in Social Sciences and a minor in Journalism. The influence that had on my children resulted in my daughter being an educator now working in Montgomery County as a Curriculum Activities Specialist for the Montgomery County School Board. My son is a board certified Surgical Podiatrist with Kaiser Permanente. I am truly grateful for the influence Mrs. Murphy's had on my life."

13.

B+A=Escape

Unsung Athletes
They ran faster than those of Olympic fame
Yet no records bare their names.
With professional skill they could compete in any game
These neighborhood legends never attained school league acclaim
In any sport they showed grace, speed and power,
The art and science of athletic skill.
These amazing athletes who could jump higher and farther
Never played in a great stadium or park.
No stories were ever written about them
Their feats are regarded, if it all, as mythical.
Those who saw them play know that few are prepared
To believe what they saw these playground athletes do.
They never played a high school varsity sport
They dropped out of school early
A few returned to the delight of coaches
Only to leave before competing in any contest.
They might have changed the faces of many sports
Had they been willing or able to stay in school.
Their talents so great on the fields and courts
No match for the forces that derailed them early and forever.
                                                    Robert M. Dixon, Ph.D.

Wes offers his observations about the importance of the recreation centers in Cherry Hill. "I want to comment on this poem that comes from a book of poems entitled, Old Themes – A Different Voice by Robert Dixon,

Ph.D. Dixon is an African American educator and a brilliant scientist—a physicist as I understand it. When I became familiar with his background, he was serving as a Provost at the first historically Black College, Cheyney University of Pennsylvania. Dr. Dixon is an intellectual, a lecturer, a scientist and has an absolutely stellar career in academia. He was also a star football player, trackman and overall notable athlete. He is an impressive man who, while I have not had the opportunity to meet him, someday I hope to because he is an example and model of what a it takes for an African American male to be accomplished and successful in American society.

"In referencing Dr. Dixon and his poetry that captures the essence of so much as it applies to the plight of people of color in America, I also recall something I heard that he said about himself, 'The past that I come from is in my bones. It is a part of me—my genetic makeup. From the era of slavery in America to the struggles that my people went through and continue to endure in various forms, that is all a part of me. I have an obligation to better myself in life and to help others.'

"For me, what rings out in that brief humbly expressed bravado by Dixon is that his background illustrates tremendous intellectual talent; yet, that alone was not a defining aspect of him as a Black man. He was also a superb athlete. Now I'm not saying or even suggesting that Black men in America must orient their attempts at a better life to being smart and athletic. Yet, I do see where it is very clear to me, as exemplified by Dr. Dixon's life of accomplishments, that brains—smarts that translate into at least a Bachelor's Degree—along with athletics, being able to perform in competitive sports, are one set of keys to success for Black males."

As we were ending our high school years, we were aware of the outside world's encroachment into what had been sublime lives. We knew that it was time to put in place life plans for which our Cherry Hill teachers had prepared us so well. The young men of Cherry Hill had additional life preparation from the culture they had been immersed in on the street corners, the front porch steps, and at the community recreation centers. There was usually an older male who positioned himself as mentor to a group of younger boys. They used their time with each other to hone their life skills. There were competitive sports being played, but there was also competitive story telling with outrageous tales of danger as well as sexual prowess. There was street corner singing and playing the dozens, a game of one-ups-man-ship to create the most stealth yet humorous insult to something or someone held in high esteem.

Wesley Pugh remembers, "The most lasting entertainment experience came when the older guys, after having drunk some Thunderbird or Boone's Farm would stand under a lamp pole in the dark of summer nights and sing—equal to and better than the greatest R & B singers of any generation. I recall falling to sleep in my bed as their songs and a cappella voices permeated the night air. No one objected to the sound. The police never stopped to tell them, 'Move on!' Their voices and harmonic melodies were unmatched. Those guys were gifted black night song birds."

The older guys also served as style mavens for the younger ones. There were two distinct groups into which they fell—jitterbugs and collegiates. Jitterbugs were the trendy dressers, usually guys that were heading off for jobs after high school. They could be seen parading on a Friday night in their starched denim jeans, starched shirts and Chuck Taylor sneakers. Collegiates were the guys who were more conservative with their style, usually sporting their letter sweaters, nice slacks and wingtip shoes. For the most part, they were headed to college.

Mrs. Dorothy Pugh sought to keep her boys out of trouble and got them working as soon as they were old enough to get their work permits. She helped Wes land a job working at the recreation center where he liked to hang out anyway, so it was hardly like working. One of the rites of passage was to watch the older guys play their pick-up games. Even though there were established times for the various age groups to play, the older guys dominated the courts any time they so chose. The younger guys didn't mind waiting for their turns because they were witnessing greatness. Then there were the occasions when the older guys didn't have enough players, and they would select a few of the younger guys to play with them. What an honor! And Wesley, a tenacious little skinny kid, had the good fortune to be paid to mop the floors at the school to which the recreation center was attached and hanging out with the guys.

The older guys took great pride in beating up on the younger ones on the basketball court. There was the time that an older guy took it to Wes. The older guy shot all over him and dribbled around him in a way that left him gasping for air and running futilely to stay with the older guy up and down the court. And then, a couple of years later, when Wes started "feeling his oats," he was paired with the older guy again. This time, Wes gave as good as he got. That was the expectation—give the older guys a double dose of the on court abuse that the "old heads" once dished out. It was all acceptable behavior, no hard feelings. In fact, there was a quiet acceptance by the older males, a feeling as if they had in some measure influenced and prepared the young now maturing athlete who was in the future going to "represent" Cherry Hill.

So it was, preparing the younger ones, sending them off to a possible stellar high school career in athletics. What often time happened years later to Cherry Hill kids, the older community guys would call out to the high school athlete, somehow mysteriously through a secret grapevine knowing who made the team and who got cut, and shout a word of encouragement. As Tupac says, "show a young brother love!" There was a deep sense of appreciation by the older guys for the younger brothers.

"The Cherry Hill recreation center was an opportunity for me to see the likes of stolen athleticism and realized successes," says Wes. "Even today, what permeates my psyche are three lasting impressions that I have taken and live with as it relates to the Cherry Hill recreation center. They are having bared witness to the greatest basketball pass ever thrown, witnessing one of the most impressive long-range shooting exhibitions ever displayed on any level of basketball competition, and learning that B+A=Escape—getting at least a bachelor's degree plus honing athletic ability as keys for a black male to escape to a better life."

As to the greatest basketball pass ever thrown, Wes remembers, "It was a rather routine autumn day, and we were either sitting on the floor or standing around shooting the breeze and watching the other guys play as we waited our turn on the court. It was a five on five full court game in progress. The players out on the court were running up and down, trading baskets—a few missed jumpers—but mostly fierce drives to the basket and a number of acrobatic lay-ups to go along with the usual disputes over who touched the ball last, was it or was it not a foul, and I didn't step out of bounds, etc.—street ball.

"Then there was this one play in which the ball lands in the hands of this cat named Raymond Rawlings who almost always played in his neatly creased starched blue jeans wearing his seemingly always new Chuck Taylor sneakers. Since he was on the tee shirts team against the skins, the shirtless team, his starched dress shirt was neatly folded on an unoccupied chair that no one dare sit in or ask whose shirt with an intent to move it. Raymond was one of the best dressed guys in Cherry Hill, both on and off the basketball court. While he had a very calm demeanor on and off the court, he was quite assertive when he chose to be. He was one of the guys who implicitly was highly respected in the community by his peers. No one wanted to ever get in a fight with Raymond or his younger brother who could fight as well as anyone in the entire Cherry Hill community.

Everyone knew, you don't mess with the Rawlings. And while both the Rawlings brothers were private and had a very calm, friendly disposition, they spoke to everyone. The main point was, you don't want to be on their wrong side.

"As I was watching this game going down, the words that come to mind will not do justice to what occurred. Someone took a long-range jumper and missed. The rebound came off the rim and into the hands of Raymond Rawlings who was at the top of the key. As he gathered control of the ball and turned to dribble up the court, he made a really nice head and body fake that left behind the guy trying to defend him. Long before the crossover move that Allen Iverson patented and made famous, the Earl the Pearl hesitation dribble was the classic playground move that included a behind the back pass, if you were an urban legend like Raymond who could imitate and duplicate the pros.

"On the play I observed, he had left the guy guarding him behind and was at breakneck speed dribbling down the middle of the court. Just as Raymond crossed center court, on his right side was a fast breaking, hard running teammate cutting toward the basket. An opposing player was running with Raymond's teammate, yet, as is the rule in basketball, as a defender you have to play the ball and stop the opponent's dribble and movement toward to basket, which is what occurred. Leaving his man, the shirtless opposition player ran toward Raymond and put his hands up in the air to both obscure Raymond's vision as well as to deflect a potential pass in an effort to protect against a fast-break basket. Seeing his teammate cutting diagonally toward the basket from the right side and the opposing player approaching him with hands in the air, Raymond leaves his feet and jumps in the air just as he crosses mid-court.

"Now everyone knows that in basketball when making a pass, the rule of thumb is that you should never leave your feet. However, in Raymond's case, being that he was always someone who lived by his own set of rules, as the opposing player ran toward Raymond with hands up and jumping in the air to match Raymond's rather unorthodox move of leaving his feet to make a pass, to ensure that the pending pass would not go over his hands or get past him, the defending player simultaneously slightly split his legs open as he left his feet in preparation to at least kick the ball if Raymond tried a bounce pass.

"With all passing lanes closed, so it seemed, as the opposing player who was slightly taller than the six foot or so Raymond, what then occurred can be described by words taken from the poem *Unsung Athletes*:

Linda G. Morris

Their feats are regarded, if it all, as mythical.
Those who saw them play know that few are prepared
To believe what they saw these playground athletes do.

"With both players in the air defying gravity, I saw Raymond Rawlings very calmly and without hesitation firmly grip the ball with both hands and in one fluid motion, while going up in the air and seeing the mirror opposition player, deliver a precise perfect bounce pass through the slightly parted legs of the defender and hit his teammate in stride as he was cutting toward the basket for an easy lay-up.

"Those of us who witnessed "The Pass," didn't even scream and shout and give high fives or react, except to be hypnotized in silence by what we saw as Raymond Rawlings dropped back on defense, in a very cool and calm manner as if nothing happened. He just had skills like that!

"I know there are great pro players and other unbelievable playground basketball legends that have performed miracles on the court. Yet, in the Cherry Hill Rec Center, on that Fall day in the mid-1960s, believe me that as an avid basketball junkie as well as a connoisseur of the sport, what I witnessed defies description, and in my mind will always be the greatest basketball pass ever."

It was in the heat of a July day that Wes witnessed the most impressive long-range shooting exhibition. During the summer, the Rec Center extended its hours because it was too hot to play outside. Wes said, "We were playing a pick-up game of basketball, five on five, without any real intensity. As we all played at less than full speed, one of the players on the team I was on got winded and wanted to sit out the rest of the game. There was no one around to take his place so in order to keep the teams even, I encouraged him to at least just pretend to guard his man and pass the ball to me. I liked to shoot! The game was progressing in a rather ho-hum fashion, when Lenny Hamm casually strolled into the gym. Now there are people in Baltimore who many years later have come to know Lenny as the former Police Commissioner. Yet, I knew Lenny when he was a celebrated basketball player who went from Cherry Hill to one of the most prestigious high schools in the city—City College, an all-male high school. Lenny later won a basketball scholarship to play at Philadelphia College of Textiles in Philadelphia, now known as Philadelphia University.

"Lenny was on summer break and had just stopped into the gym to see what was going on. I grew up with Lenny's younger brother, Tommy Hamm, who was a really good basketball player that had a nice jumper and passed the ball even better. I was on the receiving end of quite a few of Tommy Hamm's assists. Lenny watched us play, at times nodding his approval to a few of us who caught his eyes after making a basket. And then one kid defied all rules of street ball protocol by asking Lenny to run for him. Now Lenny was much older than everyone who was playing, and he was a celebrated star performer and a college player. Yet, since it was not a serious game, there were no complaints about him playing. What occurred when Lenny Hamm stepped onto the court was a thing of beauty. Lenny Hamm, at least in my book, is no unsung hero. He is a Cherry Hill hero who, to quote that poem, possessed,

'The art and science of athletic skill,
These amazing athletes who could jump higher and farther.'

"I saw Lenny Hamm in a rec center pick-up game while casually play-ing on the same team I was on, as he took a pass and just as he crossed mid-court, pull up, with perfect form and follow through, shoot a jump shot that was all net, effortlessly from mid-court. Then a few baskets later, he did it again; and again and again. His shooting performance went on to the extent that the opposing team players, I swear, were hardly trying to make a basket because we all just wanted to see smooth Lenny Hamm bang jump shot after jump shot. Witnessing Lenny Hamm put on a shoot-ing exhibition at the Cherry Hill Rec Center on a hot day in July was mighty special."

Witnessing life as played out on the basketball court gave Wes an appreciation for how athletics could serve to propel him on his journey. Wes and his older brother Phil, were steeped in this culture and knew that the same skills that they tried to perfect in their play—assertiveness, dominance, competitiveness—could take them far in transitioning from life in Cherry Hill to the world outside and a prosperous adult life. They created the formula B+A= Escape.

Phil, as the oldest brother, was a natural leader. He led the way as one of the group leaders when it came to exploration in the woods. He was always noted for having a style of shooting marbles that was fancy and deadly accurate. Phil pitched a mean softball with the speed and velocity that made opposing players rarely get hits. Yet while Phil was accom-plished on the softball diamond, he also made his mark in basketball at City College.

Coming from Cherry Hill and attending the academically demand-ing City College High School was no easy feat. Phil was also a highly celebrated long jumper and high jumper in high school and college. So Phil Pugh went on to "represent" Cherry Hill as a good student at City College High School; and a tremendous athlete who even after high school enjoyed athletic success in college, and he got his degree from Morgan State College. Soon after college, Phil had a basketball try-out with the then Baltimore Bullets (now the Washington Wizards). At the Bullets tryout camp, Phil is rumored to have held his own against a few highly regarded rookie draft picks of the Bullets. Yet, at the end of the first day of training and try-outs, he was so spent from the physical and athletic toll it took to play basketball on a professional level that Phil decided to not return to the training camp. He instead chose to pursue a career in teaching.

Wesley did not want to be defined by his older brother. Wes's game became football. Wes also seemed to take to academics very differently than his older brother. Whereas Phil was a good student, Wes always wanted to be the best student in the class. Wes chose to go to a high school that was completely different than the one attended by his older brother. After leaving Cherry Hill Junior High School, Wes decided to attend Forest Park High School, a predominantly Jewish school in north-west Baltimore. He was not about to follow Phil to high school, and hear the questions he constantly was asked in junior high, "Are you Phil Pugh's brother? Are you as good as him in sports?"

Wes decided to make his mark in athletics at Forest Park where he became a scholar-athlete and was inducted into the National Football Foundation and Hall of Fame and given the Greater Baltimore Chapter Scholar Athlete Award. He was a wide receiver on an undefeated fresh-men football team, and he also played quarterback at the varsity high school level. Wes was All-State as a safety and punt returner, a wide receiver, and a major part of the Forest Park varsity. This was an unde-feated and untied Championship team that in the over 70 year history of the school remains the best winning team ever.

Wes also played high school basketball, and he learned lacrosse from a close Cherry Hill friend. Wes went on to be awarded those All MSA (Maryland Scholastic Athletics) / All State letters in football, basketball and lacrosse. He went into the Forest Park Hall of Fame and later attended Dartmouth College in Hanover, New Hampshire, and made their Hall of Fame for Football. Wes also earned a master's degree and a Ph.D. So com-ing from Cherry Hill, the two Pugh boys more than represented. They excelled and confirmed that brains, leading to at least a bachelor's degree along with athletic excellence do serve as conduits and are two keys for

Black males to escape the stigma of being perceived as less than and not valued in the American culture.

In contrast, the youngest Pugh brother, David, was too young to benefit from the comradery of his older brothers. He never really had the opportunities to play with the older kids and to be exposed to the exploration of the woods and interact throughout the Cherry Hill Community. By the time David reached his early teens years, the Pugh's had moved to the Park Heights section of town. Park Heights was an area of upward mobility which opened up to blacks with the passage of the Fair Housing Act. Unlike living in Cherry Hill with its sense of one community, David had to learn how to navigate the inconsistent city streets and run through the rough areas to keep from getting stopped and possibly beat up for being in the wrong section of town. He adapted to that quite well. However, David never completely grew accustomed to the stellar athletic paths that his two older brothers had paved and left for him to travel.

While there were no older Cherry Hill guys to school David, he his two RICH (raised in Cherry Hill) brothers were in his life. As a result, he learned to catch a football with precision as Wes would work out and at times play football catch with him to challenge him to be the best. Phil would take him along, as he at times had done with Wes, to play basketball with the "big boys."

David saw his older brothers' accomplishments, both in athletics and in school, and he responded like a true Cherry Hill descendant. David carved out his own path to success. He attended the then newly built Northwestern High School, and during his years in high school, he was a good student and a fair athlete. He was much skinnier than the rest of the Pugh boys but, in the summer between high school and college, David gained some weight as well as grew 6 inches to 6 feet 6 inches. He became a multi-talented athlete that in many ways exceeded his two older brothers. David went on to attend what was at that time the most prestigious college in the country for physical education—Springfield College in Massachusetts. At Springfield College David was a proto-type big, tall, wide-receiver on the football team, but his sport was really basketball.

On the basketball court Dave Pugh was considered a "beast." He played with such relentlessness that he set scoring records, rebounding records, and achieved—similar to Phil—All American type honors for basketball. Dave also was a goalie in soccer; a goalie in lacrosse; and, an overall stellar athlete who also stayed at Springfield College an extra year to get his Master's Degree.

After college, Dave Pugh went to the then New Jersey Nets basketball training camp. Unlike his older brother, Dave was in shape and committed to becoming a professional basketball player. However, he soon learned that the pro game is about more than just talent. It matters who has a guaranteed contract and who was drafted and in what order (even if you are a better player than the other guys).

After being released from the Nets training camp, David went on to play ball overseas in Bahrain. In less than a year, not able nor willing to adjust to the cultural lifestyles, he returned to the states and settled in St. Croix, the U.S. Virgin Islands, where he instantly became an island basketball legend who was both admired for his skill level and hated for his on the court ferocious trash talking aggressive play and stellar performances. David convinced Phil to move to St. Croix where they both have now lived for more than twenty years.

All three of the Pugh boys went into the field of education. Before moving to the Virgin Islands, Phil was a Baltimore County elementary school teacher whom others sought to mentor into an administrator or principal. Phil resisted the notion of leaving the classroom, and moved to St. Croix to eventually marry and have a successful son and retire as a highly celebrated and distinguished elementary school teacher on the Island.

Dave retired as a junior high school physical education teacher on the island of St Croix. In retirement, he directs a boys' group home. He too married and had two daughters who achieved great heights in education – both winning valedictorian honors in high school before leaving the Island to attend college stateside and remain; one in New York City and the other resides in San Diego. Both are highly successful.

Wes also went into education, choosing not to even consider a number of invitations to attend pro football training camps. After graduating from Dartmouth, he attended Harvard University for his Masters and the University of Pennsylvania's Graduate School of Education for his Ph.D. He too married, had two greatly successful sons, and worked in the field of public education before becoming the Cheyney University of Pennsylvania Distinguished Professor in Educational Leadership. Mrs. Pugh has been heard to say on many occasions, "I am so proud of my boys."

There are countless numbers of male and female athletes and students who frequented the Cherry Hill Recreation Center and benefitted from the formula for success; others were unsung heroes who never made it out! And, then there were those who possessed brains with or without athletic talent and were able to rise-up. And yet, the Cherry Hill Recreation Center was the "epicenter" for equipping a significant segment of youth with athletic skills, prowess and intangibles that when combined with education and intellectual discipline, produced individuals who could and did obtain a great measure of success in life. They represent the best of Cherry Hill.

14.

The Bob Dylan Connection

When Mrs. Hattie Carroll left her home for work on the night of February 8, 1963, little did she know that she would not be returning home, or that she would become immortalized in song by a Nobel laureate. After all, she was only a 51-year-old Cherry Hill housewife, mother of ten children, and also a grandmother. The youngest two daughters, 14 and 18-years-old, were still living at home with their mother at 2903 Denham Circle. Mrs. Carroll was an active member of the Cherry Hill community. She was cited by the *Afro-American* for working with the women of Cherry Hill to raise $332.10 for the March of Dimes in January 1958. She also belonged to the Nous Les Filles Club, and was photographed at the club's annual gala. Another photo of Mrs. Carroll appeared in the *Afro-American* presenting a charitable gift from her club to the Anna Mae Hunter Home for the Blind. The members of the Gillis Memorial Church knew her as a stylish, hat-wearing matron who was faithful to so many church organizations and causes. To the press, she was just a poor Negro barmaid.

Nat Peacock and his family lived at 2907 Denham Circle, and he remembered the Carroll family fondly. Nat said, "Although very friendly, Ms. Hattie stayed mostly in the house when not working. Her kids were well mannered and liked by everyone. Margaret, the youngest daughter, was always in everybody's business—in a nice way—and Gwendolyn was a tomboy and didn't take nothing from nobody. But we all got along with each other like family. My brother, Earl, and Frank Carroll were best friends."

Mrs. Carroll had been hired by Baltimore's grand Emerson Hotel, which used to stand at the corners of Baltimore and Calvert Streets, on January 28, 1957, as an extra employee, working only special functions and ballroom affairs. On the evening of February 8, 1963, Mrs. Carroll was assigned to work the bar for a social event the hotel hosted annually. The event, the Spinster's Ball, was a swanky formal charity soiree, and this year the proceeds would benefit the Baltimore League for Crippled Children and Adults. In attendance this year were William Devereaux Zantzinger, a white, 24-year-old Charles County tobacco farmer, a gentleman farmer as the press dubbed him, decked out in his top hat, tails, white carnation, and cane, a light, wooden one he recently bought at a farm fair. On his arm was his wife, 24-year-old wife, Jane Elson Duvall, who also had a southern Maryland pedigree. The couple had been invited to attend the event by a Towson acquaintance.

While waiting on their wives to get ready, Mr. Zantzinger and his host went to the Penn Hotel in Towson and had a couple of beers. On their way to the ball, they stopped at the Eager House, a restaurant, where Mr. Zantzinger had two double bourbons, and Mrs. Zantzinger had five double scotches. It was here that Mr. Zantzinger started playing with his cane and playfully "tapping waitresses on the tail." By the time the couples got to the Emerson Hotel, Mr. and Mrs. Zantzinger were both drunk. George Gessell, a 19-year-old bellman, heard Mr. Zantzinger using vile language as he walked down the street to the hotel. When Mr. Zantzinger got to the door of the hotel, he yelled, "Why in the hell don't you open these doors boy?" The doors were revolving doors, and once Mr. Zantzinger walked through them, he proceeded up the steps until he turned around and saw the bellman at the bottom of the steps. Mr. Zanzinger then descended the steps, struck George on the left hip with his cane, and went back up the steps to catch the elevator to the ballroom.

Once in the ballroom, Mr. Zantzinger eventually walked up to the bar, struck the bar with his cane, and demanded service. Ethel Hill, a 30-year-old waitress who lived in the 800 block of Bethune Road, observed Mr. Zantzinger as he called the women behind the bar niggers and bitches, in an effort to get service. Mr. Zantzinger ordered a drink from Mrs. Carroll, and when he perceived that she was moving too slowly, he yelled at her, "Why are you so slow, you fat bitch," and struck her across her shoulder with his cane. Mrs. Carroll, shocked, angered and looking pale, told her fellow service staff members, "That man has upset me so. I feel deathly ill." Mrs. Carroll cried for help, immediately passed out, and had to be rushed by ambulance to Mercy Hospital where she died the next morning without regaining consciousness after suffering a massive hemorrhagic stroke.

Mrs. Carroll was not the only waitress at the Emerson who Mr. Zantzinger caned that evening. Mrs. Hill was also struck—five or six times—before and after Mrs. Carroll fell ill and was taken to the hospital. As Mrs. Hill was clearing glasses from the tables, Mr. Zantzinger whacked her across the hips. After she placed the glasses on a serving table, she got hit again, and at that point, she grabbed the cane. Mrs. Hill and Mr. Zantzinger struggled for possession of the cane until two guests separated them, and one took the cane from Mr. Zantzinger—eventually breaking it in half and turning it over to the police.

When we started writing this book, most of us did not even remember Mrs. Carroll until Charity reminded us of her. Charity told me, "Hattie Carroll's story had been tucked way back in my memory, mostly because learning of her death as a ten year old child, I could not understand why a white man would murder a black woman by hitting her with a cane. I can still recall that day in 1963 when my best friend Cheryl Redding, who lived next door to the Carroll family on Denham Circle, shared the details of Mrs. Carroll's death. Cheryl's words were unbelievable because in my mind, death was mostly associated with age and sickness. Sadly, though not spoken, death from what I observed as a child was also associated with the young men from the neighborhood who went off to fight in Vietnam where most never returned home permanently. Cheryl's brother Charles had gone off in uniform to fight in the war, and I never saw him again.

"It was difficult to process what I was hearing about the Carroll children losing their mother. When I arrived home from school for lunch the day of Mrs. Carroll's funeral and saw adults in dark clothing on her porch, I recall feeling very afraid. But of what? I could not put it into words, but the situation made me very uneasy. In my mind, I surmised that her death was somehow related to the ugly images shown in the news of whites fighting blacks over integration.

"When Linda approached us about telling the story of Cherry Hill, for some reason, Mrs. Hattie Carroll popped into my head. It had been over 50 years since Mrs. Carroll was murdered, but I sought articles from the *Afro-American* newspaper and other sources to familiarize myself with the facts surrounding her death. I also conducted online searches to uncover the details of the story that were no longer clear in my head due to the time passing. Reading the articles, I could recall the details very vividly. As a child, I had no idea that her death had become a national news story. It was during the search for news articles about Mrs. Carroll that I learned about Bob Dylan's song, *The Lonesome Death of Hattie Carroll,* recorded on Oct. 23, 1963, eight months after Mrs. Carroll's death. The article was found in the November/December 2014 on-line issue of Mother Jones, a reader-supported nonprofit news organization. I was impressed by Dylan's caring to keep this important story alive through song and immediately searched other online sites for more information about the story and the song. Although William Zantzinger received a light sentence, it was ironically handed down on August 28, 1963—the same day that Martin Luther King, Jr. delivered his 'I Have a Dream' speech in nearby Washington, D.C."

From the very beginning, it appeared to the black community that Mr. Zantzinger was being given preferential treatment. The morning after the event, both Mr. Zantzinger and his wife were taken to the police station where she was charged for disorderly conduct for hitting a police officer while interfering with her husband's arrest, and he was charged with assault, since Mrs. Carroll was still alive at the time. Mr. Zantzinger was released on $3,600 bail and his wife was released on $28 collateral. While the Zantzingers were being detained, Mrs. Carroll died. However, the hospital did not get word of Mrs. Carroll's death to the Court in a timely manner, and the Zantzingers were released.

It should be noted that Zantzinger's father, Richard C. Zantzinger, Sr., was a former State legislator who represented Prince Georges County as a delegate in the 1930s. Not to say that Mr. Zantzinger's wealth and political connections had anything to do with his treatment, but in fairness to Mrs. Carroll, they need to be acknowledged. Once the Court found out that Mrs. Carroll had died, a State-wide alarm was put out for the Zantzingers, and a warrant was issued for Mr. Zantzinger's arrest for assault on George Gessell, the bellman, and Mrs. Hill and for the murder of Mrs. Carroll. It had been assumed that the Zantzingers had returned home after the ball, but according to Charles County police, they had not and could not be found. The next morning, Zantzinger and his wife surrendered themselves to authorities. After he was arrested again, Zantzinger was allowed to post $25,000 bail.

William J. O'Donnell, the States Attorney, was already minimizing Zantzinger's responsibility for the death, saying, "From my knowledge of the law and the facts in this case, plus information from the medical examiner, this case is obviously not one of first degree murder." The information from the medical examiner was that Mrs. Carroll died from a brain hemorrhage that resulted from Mrs. Carroll's emotional reaction to being struck by the cane. The States Attorney said that the most serious charge he could bring against Mr. Zantzinger would be manslaughter which carried a maximum sentence of 10 years in jail. Blacks all over Baltimore City were upset. The NAACP, the Black Muslims (one of Mrs. Carroll's daughters had converted to Islam), and the Congress of Racial Equality all campaigned for justice on behalf of Mrs. Carroll and her family.

Zantzingers attorneys, Frederick J. Green, Jr., and Claude A. Hanley, sought and won a change of venue in April 1963 from Baltimore City to Hagerstown in Washington County—a region in Western Maryland which then had a miniscule representation of blacks. When the trial started in mid-June, the defense team, which by then had added Homer T. Kaylor, William J. Evans, and Noel Spence, opted for a decision by a three-judge tribunal instead of a jury. The judges were D. K. McLaughlin, Irvine Rutledge, and Stewart Hamill of the 4th Judicial Circuit. In his opening statement, Mr. Green denied any connection between "a friendly, playful routine tap" and Mrs. Carrol's death. He attributed Mrs. Carroll's death to a preexisting condition, her hypertension and advanced heart condition—reaching back to medical testimony from Mr. Zantzinger's preliminary hearing that Mrs. Carroll died from a heart condition aggravated by stress and strain.

At the four-day trial, Charles S. Petty, the assistant medical examiner who performed the autopsy, testified that Mr. Zantzinger's verbal and physical attacks "precipitated the increased blood pressure that resulted in a massive, fatal brain hemorrhage." While testifying that he felt that "there was a definite cause and effect relationship between the assault and the onset of the symptoms," Dr. Petty was forced to conclude; upon cross examination by Mr. Green, that Mrs. Carroll could have suffered a stroke at any time. Finally, on re-direct by Charles E. Moylan, deputy State's attorney, Dr. Petty testified that Mrs. Carroll experienced a "tremendous emotional upsurge at being placed in a position of fear, frustration, or resentment by the verbal assault, or by fear of a second blow." State's attorney O'Donnell characterized Zantzinger as playing lord of the manor presiding over the plantation. In the prosecution's argument, Mr. Moylan took the position, "We do not feel that the racial question is a critical issue and we do not intend to dwell on this. But William Zantzinger might well not be sitting in the Washington County Courthouse but for the fact that, in his inner thinking, he never accepted the verdict of Appomattox Courthouse."

The three-judge panel dismissed the murder charge and instead found Mr. Zantzinger guilty of manslaughter. At the sentencing hearing in August, they gave him a sentence of six months in the county jail and a

$500 fine for a disorderly conduct charge. The judges even permitted him time for harvesting his crop before he had to report to jail. Ironically, his sentence was announced on August 28, 1963, the day of the March on Washington at which Bob Dylan performed.

When the Reverend Theodore Jackson eulogized Mrs. Carroll on that cold, gray day in February, he sought to comfort the family and the black community that the nation was aware of what had happened in Baltimore. He read a letter sent to the family from a former Marylander who now lived in Alabama. He could never have foreseen that a young, white folk singer would feel so outraged by the murder that he would grapple with the issue of justice for Mrs. Carroll. Had we not chosen to write this book, many of us would never have known either.

15.

R. I. C. H. (Raised In Cherry Hill)

Offspring inherit, along with their parents' genes, their parents, their peers, and the places they inhabit. Leon Eisenberg

As fate would have it, perhaps just by happenstance, every once in a while in America, though it is a rather rare occurrence, public policy evolves and is implemented as government officials and politicians commit an egregious mistake to produce a positive development that highlights the achievement of societal ideals. The creation of the community of Cherry Hill is an illustration of how, in spite of a legacy of America's enslavement, institutional racism and neglect, the black community can thrive to reproduce volumes of success stories as told and recounted herein.

In June 1965, Wes Pugh was attending his graduation ceremony at Cherry Hill Junior High School. There was an overflow crowd of parents, aunts and other relatives—little kids who were related to the class of 9th grade students preparing to embark on their next academic journey. They were going on to senior high schools throughout Baltimore city after the usual summer recess. The auditorium was packed with the graduating students seated up front, along with many of the school teachers strategically placed to ensure orderliness. The gathering was a massive Sea of Blackness!

Everyone was well-dressed—as if they were auditioning for a fashion show. If they were not attired in the latest style, they were at least wearing clean, well-kept clothing as they observed on the stage one of the fellow students introducing the guest speaker for the Graduation Exercises.

While reading from a script that was prepared by the teachers, the student who introduced the guest speaker proudly and loudly spoke out, "It is my pleasure and honor to welcome one of the most outstanding football players in the National Football League. He is a player for the Baltimore Colts. He is considered one of the greatest tight ends to ever play the game. Already in his early years of playing, he has established himself as a future Hall of Fame player. It is my honor to introduce our guest speaker today, Wesley Pugh."

To the amazement and shock of everyone in the auditorium, as the six-foot-four and massively built, well chiseled handsome gentlemen walked to the podium smiling, he quickly assured the audience that was buzzing and in a state of complete bewilderment that he was not Wesley Pugh. In fact, he was John Mackey; one of the most gifted and impressive tight ends to ever play football. Years later after retirement, he was inducted into the National Football League Hall of Fame as a Baltimore Colts star tight end.

Wes remembers, "As I sat on the other side of the auditorium stage across from the podium next to a vacant chair that only minutes earlier was occupied by Mr. Mackey, I too was amazed to hear the mistake that was made by the student announcer. Yet, it resulted in a bit of a humorous retort from Mr. Mackay as he simultaneously turned in the direction of both me and the audience while stating, 'I am John Mackey, and it is my expectation that someday you will take advantage of the opportunities that will come your way to accomplish your hopes and dreams ….' Then he looked back to the audience and gave an inspiring speech, encouraging us all to strive and achieve our hopes and dreams, and to never give up fighting to overcome obstacles and the challenges that we will face in life.

"After Mr. Mackey's speech he came and sat down next to me and shook my hand as if to congratulate me for being confused with being him. As I was sitting on the stage to give the closing remarks to the graduating class, I vividly recall one of the lead teachers in the school who supervised the graduation program closing exercises going to the podium. Miss Mouton, the French teacher, stood at the podium and said, 'And now it is my honor to announce that with a grade point average of 92.8 the Valedictorian of the graduating class of Cherry Hill Junior High School for the year 1965, is Wesley Pugh.'

"In a state of mental shock and physical numbness, I recall Mr. Mackey turning to me once again to shake my hand and congratulate me, as I was asked to come up to the podium to receive an award certificate and a $50 savings bond in recognition of my academic achievement. That moment was forever imprinted in my mind. The reason I share this story is that it validates as well as illuminates something very unique about growing up and living in Cherry Hill. There are so many other students who came before me as well as after, graduates of Cherry Hill Junior High School, who were raised during their formative years in Cherry Hill and experienced it as the foundation as well as the launching pad for great successes. Reflecting back on that graduation day, it in part serves as undeniable evidence of the positive impact Cherry Hill has had on the lives of so many of this generation."

Wes recalls, "In the early 1950's when my parents moved from the segregated inner city sections of Baltimore (my father was a Korean War veteran) and a working class family with then three kids, my mother recalls the first visit to Cherry Hill and making out an application for a two-bedroom residence. She recalls how with a sense of delight she turned to my father to say, 'Wow! You think we will get one of these homes?'

"By any measure, at that time, the physically attractive qualities of Cherry Hill with its hidden deficiencies made it a community of great promise to live in and raise a family. My parents got a house in Cherry Hill, first a small apartment (at Coppin Court) while awaiting the opening for a new house on Bethune Road; and, later another larger three bedroom corner house on Bethune. Eventually, we lived in a newly built public housing project on Seamon Avenue. Somehow (someway) my mother always maneuvered to ensure that the family lived in the 'best of the new homes' in Cherry Hill.

"There was irony in identifying the newly-built public 'housing projects in Cherry Hill as the 'new homes.' During that period of time in the 1950's – early 1960's, because there was no stigma attached to living in public housing. The 'Old-Homers' as we referred to those who lived in the bungalows that first established the community of Cherry Hill before 1943, they were seen as not having the best of housing. Yet, there were no perceived class distinctions between Blacks living in the old homes or the new homes. We all got along quite well!"

The population of Cherry Hill had a very distinct characteristic based on America's housing segregation policies of discrimination. Thereby, as a community Cherry Hill was comprised of professionals – lawyers, doctors, educators/teachers, as well as working class individuals. There were also families headed by single parents on welfare. While the adults' interactions were partially dictated by educational status, there was no distinct separation between the children who lived in Cherry Hill as school, church, play/sports, and dance parties served to bridge any pronounced socio-economic class divisions among the youth.

There are statistical data that trace the median income and percentage of single parent households headed by females in Cherry Hill; and, document evidence of the formal educational levels of residents ranging from a large percentage of adults with less than a high school degree; and income levels that label the community as "low socio-economic status." Yet, the reality beyond the statistical profiles was that Cherry Hill, as a community of "like-minded Black folks," had its beginnings as a place where dreams were inculcated with hope and an implicit set of values to believe that everyone could succeed in America.

It should be acknowledged that this writing of shared experiences about living and growing up in Cherry Hill is not a memoir. The array of writings herein is an accumulation of unified voices and stories of children from Cherry Hill. These insights offer a reflection on the shared human values as well as life challenges which people of color encounter, and serves to illustrate realistic hope that seeks to inspire.

"As for my story," says Wes, "a few years afterwards, I was invited back to the school and delivered a class graduation speech in which I emphasized the then 1960's catch-phrase of the civil rights activist, Jesse Jackson, 'You Are Somebody!' Similar to every child raised in Cherry Hill, my formative development is a unique journey. Yet, it is commonplace to the extent that it seeks to honor parents' genes, their parents, peers and the place we habited during a most crucial period in our lives in America.

"Living in Cherry Hill as a child was accented by frequent visits from grandparents. I recall my father's mother (Lillian Pugh) who had real estate holdings in other parts of the city, often making visits to Cherry Hill to see her grandchildren, and in secret grandparent fashion, slip a silver dollar coin or some equally valuable monetary gift in each child's hand. The result was days of candy and junk food purchased from Daddy Logan.

"My Grand-mom's visits to Cherry Hill also had a reciprocal aspect, as each summer she would come and alternately select one of the older kids in the family (choosing from among three of us) to take on a one-week summer vacation to the beach or some tourist type location. I remember the train rides and playing in the beach sands that were similar to the textured terrain of the "mountain cliffs" we jumped off of in Cherry Hill.

"My mother's father, Granddaddy—Eddie Bishop, was perhaps one of the most unique family visitors to Cherry Hill. When he came, not with 'big money' in hand (yet you would always get a quarter or two), his visit was a marvel of tiny miracles as he would go around the house and in each room fix and repair any and everything that was broken. Starting in the kitchen I would follow Granddaddy around and watch him fix the dripping faucet. The electrical outlets were adjusted. The iron was repaired along with the waffle iron, blender and any other mal-functioning kitchen appliance. In the living room the television was returned to picture perfect condition. If there was a paint touch-up to do or wall-paper to be hung, he did it. When Granddaddy left our home in Cherry Hill, it was irrelevant as to whether the Housing Authority maintenance men came around to address any work orders. Eddie Bishop left his mark!

"Similarly, throughout the City of Baltimore, Eddie Bishop was well-known and left his mark. Granddaddy painted and wallpapered the home of Baltimore Mayor D'Alesandro, Jr. Cherry Hill Junior High School was constructed during Mayor D'Alesandro's tenure. His son, Thomas D'Alesandro, III, became Baltimore City's Council President and later Mayor. His daughter, Nancy later in life distinguished herself in the U.S. Congress as a prominent politician from California and the first female Speaker of the House. How proud we were that Eddie Bishop was so well connected. My mother recalls accompanying her father to the D'Alesandro's home and seeing Nancy playing along with the brothers as their dad, and her father talked in-between the pristine handy-man work that was being performed. Edward Wesley Bishop was "a jack of all trades" and a master of them all!

"The influence that a parent and particularly grandparents have on the lives of children is immeasurable. My Grandfather set a family standard in which education was a cornerstone of life. He was at one point the oldest living alumni of Coppin State University at the age of 100. He lived to be 103. Bishop, as he was also called, shared a life legacy that similar to those of us who grew up in Cherry Hill, inculcated values of hard work, education and protest.

"As a school teacher and later one of the first Black supervisors to work at Sparrows Point and thereafter in the factory of the Bethlehem Steel Company, Eddie Bishop also participated in U.S. government espionage plots at the Steel factory, to root out 'communist infiltrators' in the country. Along with his patriotic actions, he became known in the annals of the family history as the 'Rosa Parks' of major league baseball. One day Bishop went to a Baltimore Orioles baseball game at Memorial Stadium. He had been given a purchased seat close to the playing field. Once seated, he was approached by the ushers who informed him that, 'Negroes are not allowed to sit in these seats!' He was asked to leave and take a seat up in the far bleacher area. He refused. As the baseball game commenced, the attention of many of the fans was on the police contingency that came and escorted him out of the ballpark. The incident received enough 'quiet publicity' that it was the precursor to Baltimore and Memorial Stadium, as well as other major league ballparks throughout America, allowing Blacks to sit in the non-bleacher areas of the stadiums.

"Consistent with such defiance that becomes part of the DNA of the parents and their children, Bishop married a white woman. In the early-mid 20th century in America, living in Baltimore City and being married to a white (Polish) woman was not an acceptable societal norm. Perhaps that is the reason that my mother's mother, my grandmother, Gertrude Bishop, never visited Cherry Hill. Not that she was unwelcomed for she would surely have been the recipient of 'Black hospitality,' because related to inter-racial matters (unlike some white folks) Black people almost always are nice to you!

"Being raised in Cherry Hill and having a white grandparent had a rather subliminal impact on our psyches. There was an unconscious sense of 'white privilege' one inherits while growing up in an all-Black community like Cherry Hill that was neither realized nor exercised. Similar to the vast array of socio-economic categories of families, we were all equal regardless of parents' educational level; family income; career status.

"Yet the experience of a white grandparent unconsciously made life different. I recall spending weekends in Mommy's (as we called our paternal grandmother) boarding house that sat atop a small corner store. She lived in the Black segregated section of Baltimore City in which the homes were tenement dwellings and not slums—as designated by Henderson. It was with Mommy that I learned I could have whatever I wanted. She had 'a tab' with the corner store owner, and during my childhood stays and days spent with Mommy, I was allowed to go downstairs on my own to take anything I wanted off the store shelves. After one initial visit to the store when my grandmother introduced me to the white store owner, I was able to come in and take candy, soda, donuts, chips or whatever I desired, and then simply walk out the store saying in a casual assured manner, 'Put it on Mrs. Bishop's tab!' Imagine the entitlement that some kids could develop from having such an experience. Yet, for me it was felt and inculcated as appreciation for my grandmother's kindness and generosity.

"By the age of nine or ten when I was staying at Mommy's house, Granddaddy and she were apparently divorced, because I would only infrequently see him come by to spend a few hours with her and never stay for long periods of time or overnight. There was not much to do while spending weekends with Mommy. After a while of watching television, eating junk food and sitting on her lap to have her talk to me was not as exciting as playing at home in Cherry Hill.

"Yet spending time with Mommy infused the sense of feeling that 'the world is your oyster!' I learned through hard work you could have and accomplish anything in life. My Mother reinforced that sense of 'white entitlement' as she instilled in each and every child a sense of innate pride. So when the 1960's slogans burst on the scene with fist raised in the name of 'Black Power,' 'Black Pride,' 'You are Somebody!', it was natural for me to embrace my blackness. Growing up in Cherry Hill, I was always made to feel comfortable in my skin.

"I recall one of my sisters, Candy who is only a year younger than I, reminiscing about how she grew up in Cherry Hill and felt 'so sheltered' and once she left, she said it was like being a little lamb tossed to the world among the wolves. Yet, the sense of who we are as human beings was instilled in us all. My mother talks at times of how she would go to the downtown stores that were for 'Whites Only!' She could 'pass,' and while walking hand-in hand with Mommy and one of her white female companions, it was commonplace for my mother to enjoy lunch in stores and other locations that did not allow Blacks to enter. While growing up in Cherry Hill such racism was not immediately a part of one's consciousness. Instead, I can always remember hearing my mother's voice as she consistently told each of us kids, 'Walk with your head up. Be proud' I never understood the reason for that admonishment from my mother until years later when the Black Power Movement emphasized racial identity and pride.

"It seemed that everyone who was raised in the community of Cherry Hill exhibited an innate sense of pride and dignity. Although I never paid much attention to my mother insisting that I walk with my head held high. For me such a posture completely eliminated the possibility of finding money on the ground. And until this day, with a deep sense of pride in my walk and make-up, I still have a tendency to look down while walking and will often find money on the ground—a knack I developed in my childhood while growing up in Cherry Hill.

"Role models are always significant in shaping an individual's positive development. Growing up in Cherry Hill it was commonplace to have someone to admire. Perhaps not always the best of behaviors to emulate, yet you always knew right from wrong. It did not matter if you were raised in a single parent home or with both parents. Decent human values comprised the fabric of the community culture.

Cherry Hill

"I remember at one stage in my youth wanting to grow up and be a social worker, because it seemed to be an interesting gig to be able to come to a person's house and be 'an inspector.' Until I learned that the people going into neighbors' homes and causing a commotion, as the male figures would have to hide or abruptly leave out the opposite door, were social workers. They were trying to catch mothers who were on welfare with a man on the premises to cut off their monthly welfare checks and free government food subsidy. When I came to understand the dynamics and duties associated with social work, I instead decided a sociologist who studies people's behaviors then writes seeking to explain societal problems would be a better profession.

"I am not sure whether or not single parent homes were a norm in Cherry Hill. The government statistics suggest that there have always existed a high percentage of single family households headed by a female. Yet, a male figure in the house—a father, seemed somewhat typical to me. It just appeared that fathers were workers and always out making a living, so their presence was not pronouncedly noticeable. Except on Saturdays when for me every other week was a trip to the barber shop, and it was then that you would often see a collective of Black males in one community gathering.

"In elementary and junior high school it was considered a major accomplishment, when the teacher briefly left the room, to sneak up to the desk and look at the teacher's roll book to discover the first name of a male classmate's father. Afterwards, you would get a teasing by the other boys who delighted in calling out your dad's name. The threats by me and others to fight a friend and classmate for saying your dad's first name, e.g., Adolphus (or, Adolph -- as my mother called him) were more grandstanding then real in an attempt to stop the resulting playful laughter from classmates. Yet, there were occasions when I stood up to defend my father's first name as well as my last name – Pugh! It was teasingly pronounced by a few classmates, as they giggled while using their fingers to hold their noses with a squeezing grip, to suggest a bad odor.

"Teasing about another person's dad's name made no sense, yet it was also a quiet sign of respect. There was a lot of respect exhibited for each other. One of the most significant aspects of life in Cherry Hill was that at one's core, everybody showed respect for everyone else's parent(s). I know that a friend of mine, Perry who lived in the private homes, thought nothing of the fact that the rest of us guys admired that his dad cut hair on the side, in addition to his regular job. So when we didn't want to stand around for hours waiting to sit down before it was our turn to get a haircut at the barber shop, we went to around the corner from the shopping center to Perry's. We could escape the constant male chatter about sports, women and whispering intrigue by the barbershop male collective, wait for far less time, and pay half the price for a nice cut in the basement set-up of Perry's house.

"I also remember an event that made my father an athletic legend in the eyes of my friends, and had me stick my chest out. It was while a small group of us were playing baseball, in the adjacent parking lot next to our row homes, with a tennis ball so as not to break any car window if the ball hit one of the few parked cars that were in the lot. My dad walked out the house in his usual unassuming demur manner and was heading to his car when he saw us playing, and decided to make a slight detour to come over to us and ask the kid batting to let him take a swing. In inquisitive fashion, we all watched as the pitcher threw first one rather awkward delivery at the plate. The next pitch was perfect and right down the middle. In utter amazement, we all witnessed my dad hit the ball all the way over a distant row of homes as it disappeared from sight far behind and over the houses. My dad nonchalantly dropped the bat, without saying a word he continued on his way to the car, got in and drove off. All of us kids stood in semi-shock at the feat until a few realized we had to go find the ball. Yet, while searching, to hear the other kids brag about how far my dad hit the ball left an indelible mark of pride within me.

"Friendship and pride aside, there were also conflicts to deal with while growing up in Cherry Hill. Stone fights between the 'old homers' and 'new home kids' would sometimes break out. I remember one dust-filled rock throwing fight in front of the Coppin Court apartments, and instead of a stone someone threw a piece of glass that got me right between the eyes and produced a brief profusely bleeding cut on my nose. I left the skirmish and ran home to get it attended to by my mother, careful not to tell her about the stone fight because she, like the other neighborhood women would not hesitate to go looking for the culprits and to break it up while warning to tell your mother. I simply told my mom that I was accidently hit by a piece of glass and, I accepted the cut between my eyes that still to this day more than fifty years later is a visible scar that represents a badge of honor and courage as well as a birthmark from Cherry Hill.

"There were mini-gangs of boys who had a tendency to act territorial and made one decide to walk to the community shopping center along a path that avoided the gang. As was typical of gangs during that period, if one of the members was alone, he would usually say hi to you as your paths crossed. Physical conflicts between guys were usually simply fists fights that never involved any major violence, although there were a few known rare occasions of a gang jumping another kid, and badly beating him. Still, it was individual bullying that occurred, which made Cherry Hill a typical proving ground for coming of age.

"There are two events that stand out for me as my most pronounced bullying incidents. One occurred as a group of us boys were playing tackle football on the side of the rec center. One particular kid, who was much older and bigger than the rest of us yet a very poor athlete, became very angry at me because I kept running and avoided his attempts to tackle me. He became so upset that he even committed what is considered in schoolyard sports a most egregious act, he stuck out his leg and tried to trip me as I was running. Instead of tackling me, in his frustration he sought to hurt me by quickly extending his leg to bring me down. Somehow I reacted instinctively and merely jumped over his out-stretched leg, kept running to score a touchdown, and returned to the other side of the field to continue playing. Yet, the other kids laughed at him for not being able to tackle me while being such a dirty player. The result was that he approached me with his fists balled up and clearly ready to fight. It was not my intention to fight, especially since my chances of winning were slim to none! Still, I had no choice but to defend myself against his aggressive swings at me. I did a really good job avoiding his punches, not trying to land any of my own. After all, I didn't start the fight nor did I want to continue it. After he became frustrated at his inability to successfully hit me with his fists, he resorted to trying to kick me, which enabled me to easily grab his leg and trip him, by getting him off balance and flipping him to the ground. The other kids, particularly a few older ones who had joined the surrounding circle of spectators, realized that the fight was not fair and stepped in to break it up. They restrained him and made him go away, which he did to my quiet joy.

"I learned to defend myself growing up in Cherry Hill. In that period of time the most one encountered in a physical fight was someone you beat-up who would then respond by breaking an antenna off a nearby car and swing at you to really try and hurt you. I witnessed that a few times. Thankfully, it never happened to me. And gun violence was just unheard of during that period of time. It also seemed that boys were raised not to hit girls. It was emphasized so much in the Pugh household (where five girls were raised) that when one of us boys got into 'a fight of sorts' with one of the girls, the boy had to continually holler 'stop it' while defending himself by blocking the usually wide erratic swinging arms of your sister. Our sister Candy, who was known to be heavy-handed, would at times make you thankful that your mother was present to break up siblings' disputes.

"My lesson in defending myself came one evening in a quiet dimly lit street on Seamon Avenue that separated some of the distant old homes and the newly built family houses where I was at the time living. A close friend, Greg who was a year older than I, asked if I knew how to fight. I was maybe fourteen at the time and had not really engaged in any real fists fights so I told him, 'I guess so!'

"He then put his fists up in front of his face in a boxer's pose and while nodding his head signaled for me to do the same. I assumed a mirrored pose and then as he began to circle me, he at first softly slapped me in the face with the palm of his open hand. After he did that a few times with increasing accuracy and strength, I responded in kind. In unspoken terms, the two of us spent nearly an hour of combat 'slap-boxing' until we were both covered in blood from our nose and lip bleeding. Without much talk, the battle ended, and we parted ways. I went home and had my mother inquire about what happened, to which I responded, 'Oh, I was playing!' That was all I said as I went to the bathroom to clean-up. I learned to physically defend myself that night. The next day when Greg and I met up, both displaying red-faced bruises from the night before, we acted as if nothing had happened and walked to the shopping center together to buy some junk food.

Yet, the one time when I was about to really get beat up, I remember that no amount of slap-boxing skill was going to help me. In seventh grade a really big over-age kid decided that he was going to make an example out of me and beat me up. He made it clear in front of everyone in the classroom earlier in the day that he was after me. I would like to say that I don't know why he chose to use me as an example, yet, I knew the reason. Because I have always had a love for other's quick wit and jokes, I have a tendency to laugh out loud with an obvious appreciation for whatever my friends humorously said about someone else or even about me. If it was funny, I got the joke and would laugh. Well, when one of the kids referred to my antagonist as 'Magilla Gorilla' in a mocking fashion that was also based on a cartoon character of our day, my laugher attracted attention, and I was singled out as the one to meet him after school. He had decided he was going to whip my butt! And there was not much I could do but prepare to receive the beating, yet, at least try to defend myself. It was to be a fight between a 95 pound kid (me) and a 175 pound over-grown teenager. Throughout the day the entire school was abuzz about the impending combat.

"The fight was scheduled to commence shortly after school dismissal, and when we had walked a little distance away from the school grounds, enough to be out of sight of any adults, the crowd of classmates and others who were told of the fight surrounded us both in a circle of at least three to four deep. It was about to be a spectacle. I had no choice but to put my books down. He didn't carry books to school, so all he did was remove his jacket and gave me time to take off my coat. Just as he began his deadly approach toward me, out of the right corner of my eye, I saw the crowd of excited kids move aside and part as if Moses had once again performed a miracle before the Red Sea! Pushing through the crowd in a calm rage was my older brother Phil who immediately uttered, 'What you doing 'messin' with my brother!' And from that moment on I watched as Phil did to him what Magilla Gorilla was planning to do to me. In spite of Phil's thin yet really tall body frame, he could really fight! The bully got a butt whipping by Phil that made him turn and run away—never to bother me again. In school I learned to hold in my laughter when the other kids quietly made fun of him. I am not certain as to whether or not this qualifies as an authentic bullying incident or just a part of male teenagers' coming of age; yet, it was a time that I greatly appreciated having an older brother!

"Had I gotten beat up, I no doubt would have wondered, 'Where was the police, when you need them?' In Cherry Hill during the early – mid 1960's, the police presence was one of a community partnership of sorts. There were no cops cruising around telling kids or adults 'No Loitering.' Nor was there an obvious proliferation of crime in the community. The drugs and alcohol consumption was confined to adults. It was unheard of for teenagers to engage in any of the drug transactions that are normal in today's society. As teens there were times when someone "snuck" some wine or liquor from their parents' stash, and we called ourselves 'getting high!' Once one of the more enterprising guys spent weeks distilling a concoction that was to become an alcoholic drink which was a red liquid and smelled like liquor. Yet, no one dared to try it.

"Smoking cigarettes seemed to be anathema, and not a cool thing to do. The most intoxicatingly frightening game that us guys engaged in was to hold your breath, and let someone put their arms around you to squeeze your chest and abdomen for ten seconds that resulted in you becoming light-headed and semi-passing out! It was a euphoric feeling yet peculiar enough that it never become too popular.

"Police were a part of the community and never a real issue, though at times there were known cases of police brutality in which force was used and kids were hit by the policeman's club. One major means of crime prevention among the teenagers was the actions and reputation of a police officer named Page. In spite of his behaviors, he was actually admired by many of the kids in the community. Page, as the urban legend reveals, would be called to the scene of a crime, particularly a teenage theft, or if he heard about someone causing trouble he would approach the culprit, and say, 'I'm putting on my leather gloves, because when I whip your ass, I don't want to leave any marks on you!' And with that said, he would fit the leather gloves snuggly onto his fists and take the person behind a building to commence administering a real ass whipping! It was rare that he had to repeat his actions with the same individual, and when Page was seen in the police car, everyone moved on and stayed on their best behavior. While the actions of Officer Page are not a recommended way to control crime in the community among youth, in Cherry Hill it was a method that was effectively enforced by an imperfect police officer who was admired by many!

"Play occupied the minds and behavior of the youth growing up in Cherry Hill which as a locale was also a natural playground. In addition to nature's beauty and creations that embodied the community, playgrounds were often used as were the many green areas and childhood games always engaged the time and attention of the kids. I remember how playgrounds were used to play tag, and we would run around on the cement shaped pool structures that were never used for swimming, because it did not hold water. Yet, it had a decorative presence. On one occasion, playing tag –'its,' and in typical fashion while running atop the cement pool I jumped onto a metal fence that encased the playground area behind our 1024 Bethune Road home. Somehow I injured my ankle and broke my leg.

"My friends quickly went to tell my mother as I tearfully in pain tried to limp to the back door of my house, which was less than thirty yards from the playground area. My mother rescued me, while inquiring in an upset and angry voice, 'what happened?'

"The injury was such that an ambulance came to my house and took me (and my mother) to the hospital. In spite of the pain, as I was being taken out of the front door of my house on a stretcher, I looked down from my elevated position and saw what seemed like hundreds of inquisitive kids and adults gathered around to see 'what happened!' It was quite a site that attracted so much attention. I enjoyed seeing the gathering.

"Play was such a natural part of growing up in Cherry Hill. The kids played every conceivable game one could imagine. Hop-scotch was always popular because it just required being able to artistically draw the cylinder figured configuration and to then use a shoe heel to play. Girls always seemed to be better at it than the boys, and it was a very fun and competitive game. There was even the square shaped hop-scotch version that was on the elementary school playgrounds and duplicated in the street or playground area using white chalk; and it relied on one being able to broad-jump to various positions without your feet touching the lines. In spite of the physical demands of the game, girls often won.

"Playing marbles were almost an exclusive boy's game that was done on the dirt surface in front of an apartment house complex that never sought to have grass planted. A line-up of ten to twelve kids playing in four to five sets (three to four each) was typical and would last for hours. As did the evening game of throwing a can down the street, calling out someone's name and having the other kids hide and while one was seeking to tag another, others would try to sneak up and re-throw the retrieved can to keep a designated kid 'it.'

"There were so many games kids played, that included "Simon Says"; or, tuning your back and quickly counting to a certain number before turning around to try to catch someone moving; and, than there was dodge ball (that in later years become a prohibitive game due to possible injury which never occurred years before). There were also family games that included one's immediate neighbors' kids which entailed playing jacks, pick-up sticks, cards, toys soldiers that boys such as me played with in solitude, and girls played with their dolls.

"In the Pugh family there was entertainment that accompanied the games. The two sisters who were part of the triplets would team up with our cousin Kim, who spent so much time with us that she was another sister in the family, the three girls would put on a "Supremes" singing show, a routine that even had neighbors gather to watch when they performed outside on the side of the house.

"Inside when my mother and father would go out on dates with my aunt and uncle, Kim would join us and our brother Phil was in charge. And while he demanded strict discipline and for everyone to follow 'his rules and regulations,' which included what was going to be watched on television, what snacks were permissible to be eaten in the living room etc. (rules that were met with resistance by myself as the second oldest, so I usually went to my room to play alone).

"Yet, it was always intriguing how my oldest brother Phil would entertain the family of seven kids by inventing arcade-type games that would get you to lose your money. Just as occurs at Boardwalk arcades. Phil would set up glasses and invite all the kids to pitch their pennies into the glasses to win a nickel. The problem was that just as at the Boardwalk, the games were rigged against you. It was rare that someone would successfully land a penny in a small opening of a glass set up three to four feet away from you. Or, that you could guess the card he had in his hand with the promise of winning a nickel for your penny wager. The entertaining family games that my oldest brother 'invented' were marvelous at occupying the family of seven kids while our parents went out. Yet, it seemed that 'the house,' Phil, always won! Yet, everyone (but me because I watched) had fun losing their money.

"It is an anachronism to say that I was 'a nerd' of sorts. Such a term did not exist in the 1960's. Yet, just as play and games were so memorable in our Cherry Hill lives, for me the Enoch Pratt Free Library was special. It sat on top of a hill. I had to take Round Road, come to a fork in the street and choose to go right if I wanted to go to the community shopping center via the nicely built tree-lined blocks of houses; or, take the left barren pathway which led to the quaint building that housed the key to life—knowledge!

"My introduction to the Cherry Hill library came as a result of my mother. And with a deep sense of humility and appreciation I can state that if ever a building, structure, or room deserved to be named in honor of someone, the Cherry Hill library should recognize Dorothy Virginia Pugh! Because, for more than fifty years, beginning when I was in my early teens and I would accompany my mother to the Cherry Hill library, she would check out ten books – all 200 or more pages of novels and mystery reads. I would intellectually try to compete with her by similarly having the librarian approve me for five books to read, all due back in two weeks. While I tried to keep pace and to read my sports biographies and later critical writings on social issues, my mother would always be ready to return two weeks later to get ten more books while I was still on my third or fourth read. To this very day, Dorothy Pugh continues to go to the public library at age 80 plus, and checks out and reads on average ten books every two weeks. It all started in Cherry Hill!

"Just as the Cherry Hill library was located on an elevated plane, so too are the churches. As if to be a spiritual Mecca, throughout Cherry Hill, there are churches of nearly every faith and denomination that black folks identified with for worship.

"As someone raised a Catholic, out of a healthy curiosity, I visited nearly every church in Cherry Hill. Along with the unfamiliarity associated with the routines of how to respond, there was always a deeply rich spiritual feeling that consumed one as a result of the choir singing, the solemn Latin observances, or the emotionally charged preacher's sermon.

I confess to once attending a service in which the church was located on a hill and in a wooded area that I had to reach by following a flattened grassy path that led to the entrance. Once inside, as I quietly sat in the back of the nearly filled to capacity house of worship, I saw the congregation rise up in such jubilation and people passing out only to be caught by one another as the preacher did a spiritual dance that fueled the excitement. I was not used to such a religious site. In complete wide-eyed disbelief as to what it was that I was witnessing, I abruptly got up from the pew and quickly walked to the exit door, got outside of the building and ran through the woods to reach my own salvation. Churches in Cherry Hill almost always provided one with a deeply moving experience.

"I was as moved, yet not in a spiritual manner, as the graduating ninth grader at Cherry Hill Junior High School, when my name was called as the Class Valedictorian!

"The American novelist Thomas Wolfe wrote *You Can't Go Home Again* with the basic premise that youthful remembrances and a look back into one's past is never as fulfilling as the genesis and actual creation of the experience(s). Many have challenged Wolfe's view. The recreation of the memories of living, growing up and being raised in Cherry Hill is also an exception to not being able to understand the past in order to enrich the present.

"When I recently went back for a very brief and abbreviated visit to Cherry Hill, viewed pictures from the past and present, while there are remarkable changes, its essence can never be denied nor ignored as a unique American story rooted in Black success and accomplishments.

"There exists in today's ultra-modern society and technology sophisticated world, a human element that recognizes ACE's – Adverse Childhood Experiences, as a hallmark of each and every human's life story. Crucial to such a viewpoint is the 'expert perspective' that childhood is 'almost always a bad memory.' Yet, those early life experiences are said to be mitigated by growing up in an environment that is marked by a sense of safety, attachments and healthy relationships with others, and the capacity to reflect back on one's beginnings to construct what is termed a narrative. Not just any narrative, but a cohesive narrative that serves to provide the substance and foundation for one's mental, physical and spiritual health.

"As one of the many individuals who was raised in Cherry Hill during my youth and formative years, the one major accomplishment that I have taken away from the experience is that I have stayed Black! What is meant by that statement is, while 'privileged' to have attended America's most prestigious institutions of higher education, and to go to a black College / University, there was never a sense of intellectual discomfort or social awkwardness associated with any of the places where I have received an education or travelled throughout the world.

"Cherry Hill is to be credited with making a major contribution, along with family, loved ones, friends—life experiences that include success and accomplishments as well as adversity and challenges past present and future—to staying true to who we are as people of color in America.

"Many brilliant and genius children were born and raised in Cherry Hill. Were it not for the many civil rights activists (and our Ancestors) whose lives were taken, and the white advocates for social justice and equality, the brief opening and crack in the doors of equal access and opportunity would have continued to be closed to the lives of many of us who grew up in Cherry Hill.

"Today the community of Cherry Hill is faced with the challenge of fending off gentrification, as 'the establishment' seeks to claim the land for luxury condominiums and yacht docks over-looking the beautiful Patapsco River waterfront. It is highly unlikely the powers-that be will once again err on the side of people of color to re-establish a community that similar to its genesis, develops into a place that produces Black success stories.

"For the many of us who were RICH, raised in Cherry Hill, during the early years of its formation and growth, we developed a deep sense of who we are as citizens of the world, black folks who inevitably have experienced racial separation and, in varying and various forms, social inequities as well as societal discrimination amid American racism. Yet, we have stayed true to who we are – creations of GOD!

"The community of Cherry Hill provided individuals with a spiritual resiliency and capacity to overcome. Not everyone achieved. Not everyone experienced great success and major accomplishments in life. Yet we are all aware of the experience of being RICH! Cherry Hill was a uniquely special place, and produced a lifetime of meaningful memories that define us as Americans. It was also BLACK LOVE!"

16.

Fruit of the Vine

Cherry Hill was a fertile environment for planting the seeds that led to the achievement of so many of its first generation children. The excellent new schools, well-trained teachers, and the expectations that the Cherry Hill education establishment placed on the children and their families must be given due credit. The pace of the civil rights movement energized the community to demand their fair share of resources to develop opportunities and avenues to allow their children to compete at the highest levels. Our success, both individual and collective, was no accident. It was as much a consequence of the Cherry Hill Plan as the strategic layout of the streets.

In 2003, Judge William Murphy noted in his transcript for the Breihan history, "The output of the children of Cherry Hill is nothing short of fantastic. For instance, Cherry Hill has produced five judges in Baltimore City. No community in Baltimore City can make that claim. Twenty-five or thirty lawyers came out of Cherry Hill, eight to ten doctors, gangs of policemen, firemen, school teachers, social workers, and small business people." Without a doubt, the most well-known success story is that of his oldest son, William "Billy" Murphy, Jr. For several years, Billy and his father served as judges simultaneously before Billy left to start his own law firm. For Cherry Hill residents, past and present, Billy carries his family's mantle as its community crusader.

Billy Murphy's most recent success was his representation of the Freddie Gray family, the young man whose arrest, tragic injury while in police custody, and subsequent death sparked the 2015 Baltimore riots. Freddie

Gray's step father sought out Billy Murphy's firm—Murphy, Falcon, and Murphy. Billy's firm obtained a $6.5 million settlement from the City prior to a claim being filed by the family. Whenever the black community in Baltimore needs legal representation, the first thought is to get Billy Murphy. Baltimore's black community has anointed Billy Murphy as their guardian of justice.

Like Billy, his siblings are also high achievers. Madeline Murphy Rabb, the older of the two Murphy daughters, is a Chicago jewelry designer. Middle child, the late Arthur Murphy was a political strategist who helped launch several local politicians into office. Houston Murphy, the youngest Murphy son, is a Federal IT Specialist. Younger daughter, Laura Wheeler Murphy, also an attorney, was the Director of the American Civil Liberties Union Legislative Office in Washington, DC, for 17 years, stepping down in January 2015. In 2016, she was selected as an Advanced Leadership Fellow at Harvard University and is focusing on training 21st century civil rights leadership. Madeline and Laura Murphy were featured in an Ancestry DNA commercial for July 4, 2017, with other persons who can trace their ancestry back to the signers of the Declaration of Independence. They are descendants of Philip Livingston, a delegate to the Continental Congress from New York City, on their mother's side.

Cherry Hill's most famous son is TV personality Montel Williams. While Montel was born in Cherry Hill, his family moved from Cherry Hill in his early years to neighboring Anne Arundel County where he attended school through the U.S. Naval Academy. Montel's father, Herman Williams, was living in Cherry Hill when in 1954 he became one of Baltimore City's first black firemen. Mr. Williams worked his way up through the ranks of the Baltimore City Fire Department and City Government to become Baltimore City's first black Fire Chief, appointed in April 1992 by former Mayor Kurt L. Schmoke. He retired from the Fire Department in January 2001.

John Morris is a well-respected member of Baltimore's legal community for his commitment to equality in all aspects of the lives of the city's residents. John always jokes that he became a lawyer because our father wanted him to be able to sustain himself. One of the most prominent cases he has represented for the past 30 years is that of Eugene Colvin-el who was convicted of killing a white woman visiting her family in Pikesville. Mr. Colvin-el was convicted and sentenced to death. He sat on Maryland's death row for more than twenty years, and a week short of being executed in June 2000 when John and his co-counsel Jose Anderson, sought clemency for their client from then Governor Parris Glendening. As a result of their efforts, the fairness of Maryland's death penalty was called into question, and Governor Glendening placed a moratorium on the death penalty in Maryland and ordered a study to be done on its fairness.

Retired Judge Thomas E. Noel, is also a Cherry Hill native. He also graduated from the Baltimore Polytechnic Institute, received a B.S. from Morgan State University, and his J.D. from the University of Maryland. Thomas was appointed Associate Judge, Baltimore City Circuit Court, in 1983; served as the Vice-Chair of the Drug Treatment Court Commission from 2002 to 2005, and the Judge-in-Charge, Drug Treatment Court and Substance Abuse Programs from 2003 to 2006. He now resides in Florida.

The late Jerry C. Luck, Jr., followed in his father's footsteps and became a doctor. Jerry graduated from Edmondson High School in Baltimore. He received his undergraduate degree from the University of Pennsylvania and his medical degree from the Temple University School of Medicine. After more training at the Medical College of Pennsylvania, Jerry became an Assistant Professor of Medicine at the Baylor College of Medicine in Houston, Texas. He returned to Pennsylvania in 1985 as the Director of Electrophysiology at the Penn State Hershey Medical Center. He eventually became a Professor of Medicine.

Jerry died of injuries he suffered in a tragic bicycle accident in North Carolina in May 2015. Dr. James Spicher of General Internal Medicine of Lancaster, Pennsylvania, and one of Jerry's former students said of him, "Even with a lot of things going on, and a lot of work to be done, he would always have time to sit down next to a patient's bed and talk to them. He was the quintessential physician who took time with his patients." Like father, like son.

Joan Ellis Gaither is one of Cherry Hill's most prolific artists. Joan, best known for her wall-sized, multi-media story quilts, started out as an art teacher in Baltimore City. She was attending Morgan State University when she was assigned to do her student teaching at Brooklyn Park Junior-Senior High School in the spring of 1965. Joan remembers, "The first day when I reported, the principal said, 'We have a problem.' I replied, I don't have a problem." He went on to say,

'While we have Negro custodians and cafeteria staff, you are the first Negro authority figure here. I don't expect to have a problem with our students, but I expect to have one with the faculty.' That problem manifested itself when I had to go to the bathroom and a white female teacher blocked the doorway. I said, 'You don't know me, and I don't know you. I have a biological need that we all have, and if you don't get out of the way soon, I will have to pee on your foot.' She looked at me incredulously, called me a black bitch, but she moved out of the way."

After getting her bachelor's degree, Joan did a Master's equivalency at several local colleges and went on to the University of Milwaukee where she obtained her Ph.D. in Urban Education with specialization in Art Education. Her dissertation, "Good Intentions with Unintentional Results" was a study of visual images she found in 7 elementary schools in Milwaukee that reinforced race and gender stereotypes. One example was the alphabet strip used in the schools at the time. Joan said, "For instance, the capital M had a man in a suit with a brief case underneath it. The lower case w had a woman with a rolling pin in one hand and a pan in the other. The capital I had an Indian with a round face with a head band and a feather. We , as educators, need to be careful of the visual images we project in our classrooms." Joan's dissertation won the Outstanding Dissertation Award for the University of Wisconsin Milwaukee in 1998.

Joan went on to teach at the Maryland Institute College of Art where, in her retirement, she is endowing the Dr. Joan M.E. Gaither Young People's Studio Scholarship. Joan coaches groups on creating story quilts to document their family, community, or organizational history. She encourages story quilting as a way of documenting special events and historic ocassions. The quilts are like linear books where each patch is a page within the theme of the quilt. Joan's quilts have been exhibited all over the country, and one is even on the FBI's stolen art list.

The quilting process in itself is one of building community because Joan coaches groups to bring together their individual bits of knowledge to create their stories. Joan was commissioned to do a quilt for the Maryland Commission on African American History and Culture, the Sesquicentennial 1864 Slave Emancipation Quilt. She had groups in each of Maryland's 23 counties to come up with panels relevant to their county's participating in the emancipation process. Joan worked with a group of residents on Maryland's Eastern Shore to create a quilt highlighting the life of black Chesapeake Bay water men and women in which she incorporated parts of the life jackets into quilt panels. Journey to the White House: The Obama Quilt, documents the life of President Barack Obama from his Kenyan roots to 1600 Pennsylvania Avenue. Joan has taken an old art form and perfected it into 21st century cultural relevance.

Howard Burns is an extraordinarily accomplished musician, composer, teacher, and jazz saxophonist. Howard received his Bachelor of Music Education from Howard University and his master's degree from the Royal Conservatory of Music in Brussels, Belgium. Howard played with the band, Chocolate Rain, in high school all over the mid-Atlantic region. By 1970, the band was touring with R&B groups like Earth, Wind, and Fire, the Ohio Players, Parliament, the Isley Brothers, and the Black-byrds. He has released many CDs, the most phenomenal of which is con-sidered to be *Lucinda's Serenade*, named for his late mother.

For the past 15 years, the Howard Burns Quartet has played the Ken-nedy Center and Harper's Ferry National Historical Park Don Redman Jazz Heritage Awards. Howard has been a music instructor and director of the Frederick Community College Jazz Ensemble since 1990. He has participated in numerous jazz Festivals and Music Clinics throughout Maryland, Washington DC, Virginia and West Virginia. Howard also has a quintet and a twenty-five piece jazz band and has played all over the world.

Gwendolyn A. Burns Lindsay, Howard's sister, is an award-winning volunteer for programs relating to families and children. Gwen develops and implements creative programs and projects for students in the area of health, education, and the arts. The Herstory Program is an interactive traveling play and museum tour featuring "African American Women Who Have Made a Difference from Harriet Tubman to Michelle Obama." Students are given an opportunity to travel through history by boarding a train stopping at various towns and learning facts about famous African American women. Each student is given a bandana and conductor's hat to wear, a ticket depicting a famous African American woman, and a copy of the 1963 March on Washington for Jobs program.

Gwendolyn also developed the "Working Out on Wednesday" pro-gram, "Toning Up on Thursday," and "A Taste of Books." Her philosophy is that everyone has a responsibility to help the less fortunate and to give back and provide children worthwhile educational experiences. Gwen-dolyn shared that she grew up in a family of super stars who were chal-lenged by their parents and extended family to be the best at whatever they chose to do. Many students in Baltimore City, Baltimore County and Harford County Schools have and continue to benefit from these original projects and programs.

Cherry Hill sent off its fair share of sons and daughters to the military. One such son was the brother of Nat Peacock, Command Sergeant Major James L. Peacock, a member of the Maryland National Guard for 34 years. He received the Maryland Distinguished Service Cross, Maryland's highest military award, the Bronze Star from the State of Virginia, and the Legion of Merit, the highest peace time award for the United States.

Although he died in 1993, the Maryland National Guard honored him by dedicating the Command Sergeant Major James L. Peacock wing of the Ruhl Readiness Center in Towson, Maryland, on September 14, 1997.

Pfc. Robert C. Stell was not, I would dare say, a name that anyone in our group knew before we embarked upon this project. Pfc. Stell was a 21-year-old medical corpsman who was captured during the Korean War in 1950. At the time he was captured, his family resided on N. Exeter Street in East Baltimore, a neighborhood that was in the process of being razed in the name of urban renewal. Three years later, Mrs. Lula Snell, Pfc. Snell's mother, had no place for her son to return to when she learned in April 1953 that her son had been the first UN soldier to reach Freedom Village under the Panmunjom prisoner exchange agreement.

When the City learned of the family's plight, having a newly released prisoner of war with no home to come home to in his own country, the wheels of government began to turn and the hearts of Baltimoreans opened up to meet the family's needs. The city provided Mrs. Stell with a 3-bedroom unit at 2926 Carver Road and charitable Baltimore merchants and citizens provided the furnishings. On May 7, 1953, Corporal Robert C. Stell arrived at his new home in Cherry Hill, and later that week he was awarded a key to the city.

Nathaniel Oaks, a member of the Maryland House of Delegates, representing the 41st District, grew up in Cherry Hill on Windwood Court from 1946 to 1958. Nathaniel, a graduate of Morgan State University, served in the House of Delegates from 1983 to 1989, and was re-elected from 1994 to has continued to serve to the present. Nathaniel is a staunch supporter of education and enjoys being able to provide legislative scholarships to the young people in his district.

Salima Louise Siler Marriott Gibbs was elected to the Maryland House of Delegates from 1991 to 2007. She received her Bachelor of Science from Morgan State University, her Master of Social Work from the University of Maryland, and her Doctor of Social Work from Howard University. During her time in the legislature, she introduced legislation to restore voting rights to people with felony convictions upon their release from incarceration.

DeWayne Wickham, award-winning journalist, came to Cherry Hill at the age of eight after the tragic murder-suicide of his parents. He was raised by a maternal aunt and attended school #159 and Cherry Hill Junior High School. After high school, DeWayne left Cherry Hill to join the United States Air Force where he attained the rank of sergeant and earned the Vietnam Service Medal. DeWayne received a Bachelor of

Science in Journalism from the University of Maryland and a Master of Public Administration from the University of Baltimore. His coming-of-age autobiography, *Woodholme,* chronicles his challenges as he tried to come to terms with the hand that fate had dealt him. The former *USA Today* correspondent is currently the Dean, School of Global Journalism & Communication, for Morgan State University.

After a career as banking executive and a broker in the real estate division of Legg Mason, Calvin Thomas is a partner in prominent real estate practice in the Baltimore-Washington, DC area. Walter Thomas is now Bishop Walter S. Thomas, Sr., the Pastor of the New Psalmist Baptist Church, one of Baltimore County's mega-churches, for over 40 years.

Charity Welch, Ph.D., learned to value education before her family arrived in Cherry Hill. Her father taught his children math and science around the dinner table in their home on Bevans Street. He read them the poetry of Paul Lawrence Dunbar, Omar Khayyam, William Cullen Bryant, and others. Charity watched as her two older siblings learned to recite the names of the presidents backward and forward. It was this kind of exposure that inspired Charity to become an educator. She received her B.S. and M.A. in Special Education from Coppin State University, and her Ph.D. from the University of Virginia. Charity, who researched and wrote our chapter on education, is now the Assistant Dean of Graduate Education at Millersville University in Millersville, Pennsylvania.

Wesley Pugh, Ph.D., worked his formula of combining athleticism and education to become Department Chair and full Professor at the Cheyney University of Pennsylvania, School of Education and Professional Studies. Wes notes, "To have been raised in Cherry Hill at a time when its genesis evolved into an idyllic milieu of black people who lived their lives in pursuit of the elusive American dream that people of color know far too well as a reality, was, for many, to be rich in a soulful existence. That is the lasting impact of Cherry Hill on my life.

Terry Edmonds worked his way from School 159 to the Clinton White House as the first black speech writer. He actually wanted to go into journalism when he got out of college in the early 1970s, but those doors were not open to him. He got a job as a speechwriter to Congressman Kweisi Mfume from Maryland and moved up to be his Capitol Hill press secretary. In 1993, he became a speechwriter for Donna Shalala, Secretary of Health and Human Services. Two years later, he applied and was selected for a position writing speeches for President Clinton. By 1999, Terry was named the Director of speechwriting.

Linda G. Morris

On August 9, 2010, President Barrack Obama appointed Helen Patricia Reed-Rowe to serve as the first United States Ambassador to Palau. Palau is an island nation in the Western Pacific Ocean near Indonesia and the Philippines. Ambassador Reed-Rowe grew up in Cherry Hill, and her parents owned Reed's Carry Out in the Cherry Hill Shopping Center. A graduate of Edmondson High School, the University of Maryland Eastern Shore, and the Naval War College, Ambassador Reed-Rowe currently is a principal officer in "Embracing Next Generations," an organization dedicated to developing youth in Baltimore's inner city communities.

If you drive along St. Joseph Avenue behind St. Veronica's Church, you will come to a development of 11 town homes called Marie's Landing. They were built by Michael Tisdale, a Baltimore City contractor and community activist, and named for his mother. Michael's parents, Matthew and Marie Tisdale, moved to Cherry Hill in 1945 and lived in public housing where they raised six children on Spelman Road and Windwood Court. "My most important memory of Cherry Hill is the significance of the feeling of family," said Michael. "Living in Cherry Hill made me acutely aware of the relationship of affordable housing for ownership to the development of strong families." Michael plans to build 46 more houses in Cherry Hill.

Valerie Thomas discovered her interest in science early in elementary school. She attended Morgan State University and was one of only two women majoring in physics. After graduating from Morgan, she went to work for NASA as a data analyst. Valerie invented the illusion transmitter which produces optical illusions using concave mirrors and is used in surgery and television and video screens.

Dr. Robert L. Wallace grew up on Booker T. Drive and is the founder, President, and CEO of BITHGROUP Technologies, Inc., an information technology services company. He is a graduate of the University of Pennsylvania School of Engineering and the Amos Tuck School of Business at Dartmouth College. He says that growing up in Cherry Hill taught him that he did not want to be poor, and that Cherry Hill showed him the power of community.

If you drive along St. Joseph Avenue behind St. Veronica's Catholic Church, you will come to a development of 11 town homes called Marie's Landing. They were built by Michael Tisdale, a Baltimore City contractor and community activist, and named for his mother. Michael's parents, Matthew and Marie Tisdale, moved to Cherry Hill in 1945 and lived in public housing where they raised six children on Spelman Road and Winwood Court. "My most important memory of Cherry Hill is the significance of the feeling of family," said Michael. "Living in Cherry Hill made me acutely aware of the relationship of affordable housing for ownership to the development of strong families." Michael plans to build 46 more homes in Cherry Hill.

Michael Battle is a younger Cherry Hill resident who wanted to change the negative narrative of contemporary Cherry Hill and re-ignite the pride of its citizens. Michael has copyrighted the acronym R.I.C.H., raised in Cherry Hill, and displays it on a line of active wear worn by Cherry Hill residents past and present. Michael wants to acknowledge the proud heritage of a community that we all hope will be recognized as one of Baltimore's historic communities and experience an economic and cultural renaissance in the years to come.

These are just a few of the gifted and talented children who succeeded in spite of being sent to live on a toxic peninsula not fit for human habitation. There are certainly similar success stories about New Deal communities all over the country, but these children thrived on societal obstacles that could have doomed them for failure. This is evidence that it does take a village to raise a child, and with a solid sense of community and high expectations, any child can soar. We, the first generation, say to all the succeeding Cherry Hill generations, you have a heritage of excellence that you should acknowledge proudly. We are looking to you to continue our journey and make us proud.

Cherry Hill By The Numbers: A Demographic Consideration

Cherry Hill was a special place for those fortunate enough to have grown up there. It seemed that, for a period early in its time, Cherry Hill equipped its residents to succeed in America better than any community elsewhere in Baltimore or maybe better than most anywhere else in the United States. Cherry Hill happened to be a near all-Black community.

What exactly made the place special that goes beyond nostalgic recollection is the challenge of demographics. What it is then that distinguishes Cherry Hill from Baltimore's other predominantly Black communities?

The most obvious demographic reality that Cherry Hill embodies is that it is, and has been from its start, almost exclusively Black. Unlike the many historically Black enclaves elsewhere in Baltimore and in other cities, Cherry Hill was a planned living arrangement that happened to come into being just before the onset of the Civil Rights movement. Because of this peculiar timing, Cherry Hill emerged out of the confluence of several historic, social, and demographic crosscurrents. To understand Cherry Hill and the evolution of its demographics is to gain critical insights into the social dynamics of many other Black communities in the United States.

Understanding the demographics of Cherry Hill requires also an understanding of the social evolution of Baltimore during the middle of the 20th Century. From 1940 to 1980, Baltimore moved from just being the northernmost Southern city in America, still struggling as a racially segregated city in the shadow of the Great Depression. It proceeded through World

War II as a defense manufacturing hub, enjoying a population boom that caused a housing shortage for much of the war. In the aftermath of World War II, Baltimore encountered a civil rights revolution with the attendant expansion of its Black middle class during the 1960s and 1970s. It was during this period that Cherry Hill saw its greatest flowering of people achieving a level of success beyond the boundaries of prevailing social expectations.

Cherry Hill had its roots in Baltimore's segregated past, as, with the Second World War's winding down, city fathers dedicated space in largely vacant property on the south bank of its harbor's Middle Branch for a planned community in segregated isolation for the Black GIs returning from World War II. The segregation of Baltimore's Black population was quickly derailed in 1948 when the Supreme Court declared unconstitutional the restrictive covenant, the primary tool supporting housing segregation as a matter of law. With the holding in *Shelley v. Kramer*, landowners conveying property with restrictions against the sale of the land to a Black person could no longer perpetuate segregated housing patterns that confined Black families to certain sections of Baltimore.

The stability of segregated housing patterns in Baltimore was further disturbed in 1954 with the Supreme Court decision in *Brown v. Board of Education*, declaring the segregation of Baltimore's schools unconstitutional. The incremental drip of Black families from these early geographic confines within Baltimore City after1948, became a substantial cascade of migration in the late 1950s and then to an overwhelming tide of movement in the 1960s, particularly with the passing for the Fair Housing Act in 1968.

The demographics of Baltimore City were affected even more by the unrest that followed the assassination of Rev. Martin Luther King, Jr., in April 1968. With the destruction of many small businesses owned in most instances by White people with the resulting fear that unrest generated among much of Baltimore's White population, the flight of Whites from Baltimore's neighborhoods accelerated.

The 1950 census placed Baltimore's population at 949,706, the sixth largest city in the United States, its highest point at any census in the 20th Century. At this time, Baltimore's White population numbered 723,655 (76.20%), while its Black population numbered 225,099 (23.70%). By the time of the 1980 census, the City's population had shrunken to 786,775, the 10th largest American city, with its White population now totaling 343,113 (43.61%), and its Black population at 431,151 (54.80%), for the first census in the majority.

During these decades, Baltimore City was shaped – or by some accounts torn apart – by the following developments:

- Pre-war and post war racial, ethnic, and religious segregation of housing
- The post-war development of open space in the suburbs driving an outmigration particularly of financially successful people from more confined traditional urban environments
- The pre- and post-war immigration of new residents from Eastern Europe, particularly displaced Jews, often connecting with Jewish relatives already living in Baltimore, very often in restricted areas adjacent to areas where Black families were permitted to buy
- The readiness of families in these areas once permitted to Jews to sell to Black families, sometimes despite restrictive covenants
- The movement of Black families from their residential restrictions previously enforced by now unconstitutional restrictive covenants to areas now vacated by White households moving outward
- The flight of additional White families from areas with the arrival of new Black residents
- The aging of communities, as maturing residents remained in areas they had historically occupied while their incomes remained static or declined
- The 'Redlining' of areas where new Black residents arrived, escalating housing values for new Black families and enabling some aging White residents to relocate
- The expansion of the Baltimore's Black population while its White population declined, as Black families moved where White families had vacated, and more Black families occupied the areas that Black families had left
- The movement of manufacturing outside Baltimore, to surrounding suburbs, and last ultimately out of the area altogether
- The association of prevailing poverty with Baltimore's Black majority population.

Against this backdrop, Cherry Hill came to be. What and how it came to be requires an understanding of the demographic context of the other Baltimore neighborhoods shaped by these same conditions.

This demographic analysis examines Cherry Hill from the standpoint of the comparative evolution of the census tract comprising Cherry Hill in 1950 relative to about 17 other Baltimore tracts.[1]

Cherry Hill in the 1950 Census

By 1950, Cherry Hill had been established for just a few years. The community occupying Census Tract 25-02A sat on the south bank of the Middle Branch of the Patapsco River. In the 1940 Census, this same geographic area had reported no population at all. The 1950 Census reported a population for Cherry Hill of 6,895, of which 6,845 (99.27%) were Black.

Of the population 14 years and older, 48.67% were reported as employed at some point during the preceding year, supporting a median household income of $2,239.00, or 79.48% of the Baltimore median. The income reflected by Cherry Hill households exceeded the median income of the other sampled predominantly Black census tracts, and the home values also exceeded those in the other predominantly Black tracts.[2]

Cherry Hill managed to sustain both higher household incomes and higher home values than these other all-Black tracts, despite having a smaller percentage of its 14 year-old-and-older population employed. Cherry Hill's 48.67% employed lagged far behind the 58.60% of the West Sandtown tract employed, the 58.32% of Lower Sandtown tract employed, the 56.24% of Lower Sandtown tract, and the 52.54% of Sandtown-Winchester tract.

Even here, Cherry Hill's numbers offer an intriguing paradox. It managed this higher median income and median home value with a figure for female employment, 26.38% comparable to female employment figures for the much higher earning predominantly White tracts, Lower Homeland, Upper Homeland, Roland Park, and the still predominantly White Coppin Heights-Mondawmin tract in 1950.[3]

A more intensive review of the numbers shows that, despite having the higher median incomes, the other predominantly Black tracts sampled by far had the larger share of their populations occupying the lowest three income segments reported in the Census.[4]

In general, the 1950 census portrays Cherry Hill as a community of working families, modestly educated, raising households full of young children. Of the population 14 years and older counted as employed, nearly 35% fell within the skilled categories of "Craftsman" and "Operatives and Kindred Workers." Of the population age 25 and older, more than 55% had never attended any grade of high school, while only 2% had completed college.

Cherry Hill was a community of young children. The children under 14 represented more than 40% of the population while adults age 25 and over comprised just 43% of the population. Of the population age 14 and over, more the 76% were married.

In the larger context of Baltimore in 1950, the size of Cherry Hill's skilled blue collar work force was the largest proportionately of any of the predominantly Black census tracts sampled.[5] Its married population age 14 and over translated in more than 83% of Cherry Hill's households comprising married couples in their own household. That percentage placed Cherry Hill in the second highest position of all 18 tracts sampled in this analysis. [6]

The Cherry Hill of 1950 was an all-Black community whose employment make-up, in terms of its skilled blue collar workers, shared more in common with the ethnic all-White working class communities in Canton, Patterson Park and Highlandtown than with the other sampled all-Black tracts in and around Sandtown. However, much of Cherry Hill's social and family profile was not unlike that in the tracts with higher percentage of foreign born residents, such as Lower Greenspring (26.11%), Lower Park Heights (24.15%), Coppin Heights/Mondawmin (19.27%), Ashburton (12.82%), and Hanlon Park (12.66%). Despite the similar family profiles, these communities are heavily white collar in their work force, high achieving in educational background, and these communities uniformly supported higher percentages of home ownership, property values, and incomes than the City as a whole.

While the general profile of family life in Cherry Hill, with its predominance of married families, compared favorably with the profiles of a number of other largely White communities in Baltimore, the predicament of families in Cherry Hill was understandably different, given the disparity of economic opportunity racially. Those differences in income, work situations, housing, and housing value are apparent from the above table.

However, its geographic isolation and unique history distinguish Cherry Hill from Baltimore's existing Black communities, also segregated. These differences can be seen from the Table below together with other considerations that all the predominantly Black tracts had in common.

Compared to the other predominantly Black tracts sampled in this analysis proximate to the Sandtown-Winchester communities, Cherry Hill in 1950 was younger, populated by more skilled workers, burdened by fewer of the City's poorest residents, and favored by higher property values with a larger percentage of home-owners. In its geographic isolation and with its unique community history as a newly established community, Cherry Hill was better positioned to grow, with the expansion of economic opportunity to black residents, to retain that growth within its

Table 1

Metric	Cherry Hill	Balto. City	Lower Greenspr.	Lower Park Heights	Coppin Heights/ Mondaw'n	Ashbur'n	Hanlon Park
% Age 14 and over Married	76.01%	64.95%	64.07%	67.12%	67.93%	75.13%	71.45%
% Households Married Couples with own Household	83.70%	72.09%	82.41%	93.22%	76.82%	83.37%	83.22%
% Children Under 14	40.58%	22.50%	18.41%	20.52%	20.88%	23.80%	20.17%
Ratio of Adults over Age 25 and over to Children under Age 14	1.08	2.74	3.75	3.23	3.30	2.64	3.47
% College Educated	2.04%	5.38%	4.16%	3.94%	12.66%	11.39%	10.00%
% Men Age 14 and over employed	73.45%	75.01%	78.28%	77.74%	80.15%	85.59%	85.51%
% White Collar Employed	13.04%	41.46%	71.97%	68.13%	87.12%	87.54%	77.05%
% Population in Highest Three Income Segments	0.30%	11.38%	15.96%	15.38%	23.24%	36.23%	24.45%
Median Household Income	$2,239	$2,817	$3,387	$3,597	$4,083	$5,080	$4,250
Median Home Value – Owner Occ.	$6,443	$7,113	$8,236	$7,434	$9,885	$13,990	$10,626
% Homes Owner Occupied	30.73%	51.66%	68.13%	68.84%	50.20%	63.12%	67.99%

Table 2

Metric	Cherry Hill	Balto. City	Sandtown - Winch'er	Lower Sandtown	Middle Sandtown	West Sandtown
% Black	99.27%	23.70%	97.81%	99.18%	99.52%	98.69%
% Age 14 and over Married	76.01%	64.95%	61.25%	61.51%	61.41%	63.85%
% Households Married Couples with own Household	83.70%	72.09%	64.69%	54.79%	62.10%	72.61%
% Children Under 14	40.58%	22.50%	29.86%	19.48%	25.25%	25.74%
% Adults 25 Years of Age and Older	43.80%	61.68%	53.33%	66.82%	57.07%	57.56%
Ratio of Adults Age 25 and over to Children under Age 14	1.08	2.74	1.79	3.43	2.36	2.24
% College Educated	2.04%	5.38%	1.82%	4.44%	1.54%	1.35%
% Never to Have Attended HS	55.01%	56.44%	69.43%	66.40%	74.56%	70.23%
% Men Age 14 and over employed	73.45%	75.01%	68.22%	72.17%	71.52%	74.50%
% Females Age 14 and over employed	26.38%	33.05%	36.97%	46.07%	42.87%	44.41%
% White Collar Employed	13.04%	41.46%	15.36%	16.66%	11.01%	11.04%
% Skilled Blue Collar Employed	34.91%	35.77%	26.96%	9.39%	23.62%	31.31%
% Unskilled Blue Collar Employed	52.05%	11.93%	57.68%	60.44%	65.28%	57.65%
% Population in Lowest Three Income Segments	28.79%	26.19%	38.77%	45.10%	41.62%	37.04%
Median Household Income	$2,239	$2,817	$1,890	$1,707	$1,791	$2,042
Median Home Value – Owner Occ.	$6,443	$7,113	$5,197	$6,338	$5,336	$6,008
% Homes Owner Occupied	30.73%	51.66%	18.46%	20.85%	18.97%	25.32%
Median Monthly Rent	$35.30	$40.60	$31.07	$34.74	$31.59	$37.17

confines, and to stabilize the communities around its foundation of young two-parent families.

Cherry Hill in the 1960 Census

By the end of the 1950s, the experiment that was Cherry Hill emerged from the era of legally enforced segregation responsible for its establishment as an all-Black enclave on the outskirts of Baltimore for the returning Black veterans of World War II. However, by 1960, Baltimore had not yet assured the promise extended by the far-reaching decision of the Supreme Court in *Brown v. Board of Education*.

By 1960, Black Baltimore was no longer tied legally to the geographic confines that had limited housing opportunities to certain historical neighborhoods. For those Black families that could afford the move and weather the social challenge, the late 1950's saw the beginning of a migration of Black families physically beyond the geographic confines of former all-Black neighborhoods and socially into the middle class.

In Cherry Hill, because of its geographic isolation, social progress for many families did not require migration. Left to their own decision-making, the residents of Cherry Hill were positioned to define their own success within their own community. However, the residents of Cherry Hill were not left to their own decision-making regarding the future of their own community.

The 1960 Census reflected the prodigious growth of the Cherry Hill community at a time when, for the first time in the 20th Century, Baltimore City lost population. In 1960, the population of Baltimore City was 939,024, reflecting a net loss of just 10,682 residents in 10 years. However, the loss of population was far more dramatic.

In 10 years, the White population of Baltimore City went from 723,655 in 1950 to 610, 208, a net loss of 113,047 White people. During the same 10 years, Baltimore's Black population went from 225,099 to 325,589, a net increase of 100,490 Black people.

That population swing resulted in the transformation of many Baltimore communities. Strangely enough, one of the communities significantly changed was one that already was almost exclusively Black, Cherry Hill. The population of Cherry Hill went from 6,895 in 1950 to 13,526, an increase of more than 96%, almost doubling in population. In a community where 40.58% of the population was already under age 14, more than half of its 6,631-person increase in population comprised children under 14 (3,958).

This 10-year expansion also increased the number of residents occupying the bottom three income categories reflected by the census. In 1950, only 475 families fell within these bottom three segments. By 1960, these poorest ranks had swelled to 1,054 families, more than doubling the total from 1950. These families among the poorest three census categories accounted for 63.07%, nearly two thirds, of the families added over the ten years since 1960.

As the population in Cherry Hill nearly doubled in 1960, the census saw a decline in the percentage of men age 14 and older counted as employed from 73.45% of this segment of the population in 1950 to 66.22% in 1960. Despite this obvious influx of families and children trapped at the economic bottom, the 1960 census nonetheless documented the following developments:

- The number of skilled blue collar workers among the employed increased from 672 in 1950 to 921 in 1960 – an expansion of 37.05%
- The number of unskilled blue collar workers among the employed declined from 1,002 in 1950 to 974 in 1960 – shrinking by 2.79%
- The number of workers employed in white collar occupations increased from 251 in 1950 to 459 in 1960 – an increase of 82.87%
- While those families in the lowest three income categories rose from 475 in 1950 to 1,054 in 1960 (an increase of 121.89%), the number of families in the highest three income categories also expanded from 5 in 1950 to 153 in 1960 (an expansion amounting to 2,960.00%)
- While the number of residents age 25 and older who had never attended high school increased from 1,620 in 1950 to 2,295 in 1960, an increase of 41.67%, the size of the same population segment that had completed college increased from 60 in 1950 to 114 in 1960, an increase of 90.00%.

Apparently, the demographics of Cherry Hill from 1950 to 1960 were dynamic. Indeed, the demographics of Baltimore during this same time were wildly in flux. Its White population began to flee the City while expanses of Black people came to find a home there. How these dynamics played out in Cherry Hill is critical to understanding the social dynamics inside Cherry Hill and how it worked as a community.

The demographic analysis undertaken here respecting the sampled tracts from Baltimore begins to reflect these dynamics. While the Black population of nearly all-Black Cherry Hill nearly doubled from 1950 to

1960, in most of the other sampled census tracts, the population declined in 1960.[7]

A review of the population changes in the several sampled census tracts from 1950 to 1960 reveals differing kinds of population change. How these tracts changed over this period provides critical context to what was happening in Cherry Hill.

The predominantly White, blue collar, ethnic tracts of Patterson Park, Upper Canton, and the two Highlandtown Tracts remained racially stable. Indeed, according to the 1960 census, while the City's Black population in 1960 had grown by almost 45% in ten years, there were no Black persons at all reported for either the Upper Canton or Patterson Park tracts, while Upper Highlandtown went from 3 to 2 Black persons. The loss of population in these tracts was consistent with the rate of White population loss generally in the City – -15.62%. The experience in these tracts obviously has little to inform what was happening in Cherry Hill.

Similarly, the experience of the upscale predominantly White communities in Lower Roland Park, Gilford, and the two Homeland tracts reflect the stability of the tracts' White majority population. These tracts remained predominantly White from 1950 to 1960 and saw none of the -15.62% decline in White population experienced by the City generally. Upper Homeland, the farthest removed of the sampled tracts from the City's center. Other than Cherry Hill, Upper Homeland was the only one of the 18 sampled tracts to see any net growth in population from 1950. The tract saw growth at a rate of nearly 10%.

The grouping of tracts that offers the most salient insights about what was going on in Cherry Hill were (1) the formerly all Black tracts in 1950 around Sandtown that consistently lost population by as much as 20% and 30% while the City's Black population grew by almost 45%; and (2) the formerly all-White tracts in 1950 that, by 1960, were gaining significant Black residents, while many of their former White residents fled.

Looking variously at the tracts losing significant Black population, Sandtown, Middle Sandtown, Lower Sandtown, and West Sandtown, the formerly all-White tracts now gaining significant new Black population by 1960, Coppin Heights/Mondawmin, Hanlon Park, Ashburton, and last considering the growth of the Black population in Cherry Hill, the data begs several questions.

- Where did the Black people who left the Sandtown tracts during the 1950s go?
- Why did they leave?

- Did they migrate to the former all White tracts like Coppin Heights/ Mondawmin, Hanlon Park, and Ashburton?
- Did they go to Cherry Hill?
- If they did not go to Cherry Hill, why not?

Table 3

Metric	Cherry Hill	Balto. City	Coppin Heights/ Mondaw'n	Hanlon Park	Ashbur'n
Change in White Population	-42	-113,047	-1,395	-2,194	-2,831
Change in Black Population	+6,631	+100,490	+1,163	+2,725	+2,111
Occupied Dwellings Change	+1,247	+6,875	- -120	+82	-68
Owner Occupied Dwellings Change	+185	+10,867	-39	+46	-16
Renter Occupied Dwellings Change	+1,062	-3,992	-81	+36	-52
Percent Owner Occupied 1950	30.37%	51.66%	50.20%	67.99%	63.12%
Percent Owner Occupied 1960	23.71%	54.31%	53.67%	66.83%	64.18%
Percent Black Owner Occupied 1950	28.86%	24.01%	0.00%	66.67%	0.00%
Percent Black Owner Occupied 1960	23.66%	34.44%	61.82%	68.97%	64.08%
Black Occupied Rental Units – 1950	1,083	39,651	126	233	1
Black Occupied Rental Units -- 1960	2,152	52,749	125	232	222
Median Home Value 1960	$8,100	$9,000	$12,400	$12,200	$13,600
Median Rent 1960	$58.00	$64.00	$77.00	$95.00	$93.00

The tract data on housing may provide some evidence to answer these questions. The housing data for Cherry Hill reveals that while its housing expansion from 1950 to 1960 added about 1,250 occupied units, fewer than 200 of these units were owner occupied. The balance, more than 1,000 of the new housing units established were renter occupied. The median monthly rent for the Cherry Hill tract in 1960 was $58.00 (1959 dollars).[8]

The housing data for the former all-White tracts of Coppin Heights/ Mondawmin, Hanlon Park, and Ashburton reflect a different outcome. Here the high owner occupancy rate and low non-white rental numbers suggests that most Black families arriving to change the racial composition of these tracts were home owners of comparatively upscale residences. The Black families who arrived in these tracts were very different from the Black families who expanded the population of Cherry Hill in the 1960s.

The question then is where these Black families came from to increase the population of Cherry Hill. Given the size of the added rental population and the apparent expansion of Cherry Hill's poorest income categories, that much of the population growth of Cherry Hill in the by 1960 resulted from expansion of the public housing population by the Housing Authority of Baltimore City.

Still, Cherry Hill sustained its capacity to support social progress for residents who advanced to White collar occupations or expanded its skilled blue collar ranks, adding to the size of it highest three income categories. Despite the influx of the poorest of residents. Cherry Hill still maintained its social presence to support families. The 1960 Census reveals that 72.44% of the children under 18 in Cherry Hill were living with both parents.[9]

However, in 1960, this 72.44% figure only made Cherry Hill favorable in only a comparison with the other formerly all-Black tracts from 1950. It no longer exceeded the numbers associated with the other sampled tracts.

With the near doubling of its population by 1960, Cherry Hill faced a particular social challenge regarding its own young people. The ratio of adult age 25 and older to children under age 14 had fallen even lower than where it had been in 1950, when it led all the sampled tracts in this regard. In 1950, that ratio was 1.08. By 1960, it was 0.69, meaning that Cherry Hill was becoming a community of children and increasingly absent adults.

Could it sustain itself as a stable community through 1970 as it had managed through the 1950s?

Cherry Hill in the 1970 Census

Over the next 10 years, the racial migration of Black families from the historically restricted neighborhoods accelerated, and the flight of White families from the city continued, proceeding even faster after the April1968 disturbances in Baltimore following the assassination of Rev.

Martin Luther King. Congress passed the Fair Housing Act in 1968, and created a separate department of Housing and Urban Development.

By 1970, the Census showed that Baltimore had declined in population from 939,024 in 1960 to 905,759. Since 1950, Baltimore had fallen from the 5th largest city to the 6th largest in 1960, and eventually to the 7th largest in 1970. While Baltimore City showed a 10-year overall decline of 3.54%, Baltimore Standard Metropolitan Statistical Area, comprising Baltimore City and the surrounding predominantly White counties, Baltimore County, Howard County, Anne Arundel County, Carroll County, and Harford County, grew from 1,727,023 to 2,070,670, an overall growth of more than 19%.

In Baltimore, from 1960 to 1970, the White population went from 610,608 to 479,837, a decrease of 130,771 White persons, duplicating the loss of White population the City had sustained from 1950 to 1960, and adding another 17,724 people. During the same 10-year period, Baltimore City's Black population went from 325,589 in 1960 to 420,210 in 1970, adding a net 94,621 Black people by 1970 to the net 100,940 people increasing Baltimore's Black population in 1960.

The population of the 1960 Cherry Hill tract, 25-02A, increased from 13,526 to 14,166, stabilizing a rate of growth of 96.17% from 1950 to 1960, to a rate of growth from 1960 to 1970 of just 4.73%. However, the more significant change for Cherry Hill that the 1970 Census brought about was not in population, but in the collection of census data.

In the conduct of the 1970 Census, the single tract which Cherry Hill had occupied for the 1950 and 1960 Census was subdivided into 4 separate tracts. The analysis of those several Cherry Hill Tracts will show the transformation of Cherry Hill by 1970 into two differing communities: (1) a community of possibility reflecting the aspirations of the returning GIs from the Second World War who shaped that community during the late 1940s and 1950s, and (2) a community of neediness, largely shaped by the expansion of that new community during the latter part of the 1950s, the 1960s, and thereafter. That examination of Cherry Hill will show much more than what happened in Cherry Hill. It will reveal in Cherry Hill both the Baltimore that might have been and the Baltimore that would become in the decades ahead.

In 1970, the Census subdivided Cherry Hill into the following separate tracts: 2502.1, 2502.1, 2502.3, and 2502.4.[10] The first three subdivisions embraced those portions of Cherry Hill closest both to the water and to downtown Baltimore, Tract 2502.4 comprised the portion of the community farthest removed from the water and downtown.

Tract 2502.04 was the most populous of the four Cherry Hill census tracts in 1970. In 1970, the Census showed it with a population of 7,924, while Tract 2502.01 was reported having 1,272 residents, Tract 2502.02, had 1,220, and Tract 2505.03 numbered 3,750.

Overall, Tract 2502.04 also happened to be the poorest of the four Cherry Hill tracts, the least educated, and most under-employed, and the area with the greatest number of renters as opposed to home owners. A more detailed comparative analysis of the four tracts, together with an integration of the data for Cherry Hill as a whole community in 1970, is set forth in the table below.

Table 4

Metric	2502.01	2502.02	2502.03	2502.04	Cherry Hill
Population	1,272	1,220	3,750	7,924	14,166
Population Under Age 14	483	359	1,228	3,843	5,913
Population Age 25 and Over	516	527	1,669	2,217	4,929
% Population Under 14	37.97%	29.43%	32.75%	48.50%	41.74%
% Adults 25 Years of Age and Older	40.57%	43.20%	44.51%	27.98%	34.79%
Ratio of Adults Age 25 and over to Children under Age 14	1.07	1.47	1.36	0.58	0.83
% of Population Age 14 and over married not widowed, living apart or divorced	72.88%	66.78%	67.05%	42.59%	55.48%
% of Children under 18 Living with Both Parents	61.45%	76.02%	70.00%	29.66%	63.53%
% of Children under 18 Living with Mother Alone	34.84%	8.78%	16.42%	63.53%	48.29%
% College Educated	16.27%	4.17%	3.06%	0.90%	3.61%
% Never to Have Attended HS	17.44%	31.12%	39.13%	49.98%	40.88%
% Men Age 14 and over employed	82.61%	85.67%	77.44%	56.50%	70.36%
% Females Age 14 and over employed	63.84%	51.06%	56.77%	37.28%	46.68%
% White Collar Employed	38.25%	41.65%	30.40%	28.95%	32.24%

(Continued)

Metric	2502.01	2502.02	2502.03	2502.04	Cherry Hill
% Skilled Blue Collar Employed	42.71%	39.24%	38.70%	31.39%	36.57%
% Unskilled Blue Collar Employed	18.35%	18.91%	29.20%	39.04%	30.20%
% Population in Lowest Three Income Segments	3.61%	2.56%	10.76%	37.38%	22.76%
% Population in the Three Highest Income Segments	6.56%	16.97%	7.57%	3.93%	5.87%
Median Household Income	$8,891	$9,643	$8,517	$3,869	
Median Home Value – Owner Occ.	$15,600	$9,400	$8,400	$7,000	
Occupied Dwellings	406	332	1,079	1,764	3,581
% Occupied Dwellings Owner Occupied	3.67%	40.06%	26.14%	7.82%	15.86%
Renter Occupied Dwellings	391	199	797	1,626	3,013
Median Monthly Rent	$93	$107	$82	$64	

The above demographic profile of the four Cherry Hill tracts reveals little that clarifies developments in Cherry Hill. While Tracts 2502.01, 2502.02, and 2502.03 seem uniformly different from 2502.04, in terms of numbers, youth, wealth, and family makeup this tract sustained more than $6,000 lower than the home values in Tract 2502.01.

A consideration of the demographic shifts in the other sampled tracts in Baltimore may give context for understanding Cherry Hill. As was the case with the 1960 Census, 1970 saw further migration of Black families into neighborhoods formerly restricted by race. Of the 18 1950 Census tracts sampled for this demographic analysis, of which 5 were then predominantly Black, by 1970 the predominantly Black tracts numbered 10. Beyond the original 5 predominantly Black tracts, the 1970 Black tracts additionally comprised Coppin Heights/Mondawmin and Hanlon Park, which tracts had increased their Black majority populations from 1960, together with Ashburton, Lower Park Heights, and Lower Greenspring. In each of these 10 tracts, the percentage of the population that was Black exceeded 94% of the population.

The other 8 sampled tracts that were near exclusively White remained that way in 1970. The 1970 profiles of these all white tracts are set forth in the table below.

Table 5

Metric	Upper Canton	Patterson Park	Lower Roland Park	Guilford	Upper Highland-town	Lower Homeland	Upper Homeland
Population	4,744	4,606	4,332	8,530	3,973	4,435	6,975
Population Under Age 14	849	559	636	740	778	609	1,337
Population Age 25 and Over	3,110	2,075	3,447	5,503	2,459	2,741	4,551
% Population Under 14	17.90%	17.67%	14.68%	8.68%	19.58%	13.73%	19.71%
% Adults 25 Years of Age and Older	65.56%	65.60%	79.57%	65.51%	61.89%	61.80%	65.25%
Ratio of Adults Age 25 and over to Children under Age 14	3.66	3.71	5.42	7.44	3.16	4.50	3.40
% of Population Age 14 and over married not widowed, living apart or divorced	57.95%	56.11%	51.14%	37.84%	61.10%	49.27%	60.82%
% of Children under 18 Living with Both Parents	74.76%	76.95%	84.70%	69.16%	77.14%	87.04%	89.68%
% of Children under 18 Living with Mother Alone	12.97%	9.11%	6.50%	16.96%	11.19%	7.53%	6.79%
% College Educated	1.41%	0.82%	33.07%	27.44%	1.83%	35.35%	35.40%
% Never to Have Attended HS	57.40%	67.04%	15.35%	21.08%	59.09%	16.93%	12.70%

% Men Age 14 and over employed	73.30%	72.47%	73.92%	51.45%	65.52%	65.69%	73.60%
% Females Age 14 and over employed	31.39%	36.98%	36.29%	43.57%	35.78%	38.89%	38.39%
% White Collar Employed	86.32%	78.58%	35.57%	74.78%	84.20%	32.14%	43.56%
% Skilled Blue Collar Employed	6.24%	10.58%	49.12%	12.83%	6.02%	49.69%	42.69%
% Unskilled Blue Collar Employed	7.44%	10.64%	15.31%	12.39%	7.79%	17.86%	13.75%
% Population in Lowest Three Income Segments	2.48%	3.68%	13.02%	7.97%	4.48%	15.78%	8.02%
% Population in the Three Highest Income Segments	66.53%	49.68%	16.65%	23.90%	61.93%	12.96%	14.49%
Median Family Income	$21,085	$14,930	$9,087	$9,083	$19,658	$7,772	$9,414
Median Home Value – Owner Occupied	$34,900	$28,600	$7,800	$32,100	$10,500	$6,900	$8,600
Occupied Dwellings	2,320	1,566	1,463	4,414	2,387	1,198	1,745
% Occupied Dwellings Owner Occupied	80.26%	41.89%	67.87%	16.06%	23.42%	72.87	73.52%
Renter Occupied Dwellings	458	910	470	3705	1,828	325	462
Median Monthly Rent	$111	$156	$82	$171	$101	$70	$76

Table 6

Metric	Coppin Heights-Mondawmin	Lower Greenspring	Hanlon Park	Lower Park Heights	Ashburton
Population-1970	2,192	7,791	2,842	7,927	9,338
Population Change from 1950-1960	+128	-193	+635	-810	-714
Population Change from 1960-1970	-230	+1,700	-102	+2,304	+1,661
Population Change from 1950-1970	-102	+1,507	+533	+1,494	+947
White Population Change from 1950-1960	-1,395	-505	-2,194	-1,447	-2,831
White Population Change from 1960-1970	-814	-5,464	-130	-4,520	-5,136
White Population Change from 1950-1970	-2,209	-5,969	-2,324	-5,997	-7,967
Black Population Change from 1950-1960	+1,163	+302	+2,725	+653	+2,111
Black Population Change from 1960-1970	+943	+7,162	+24	+6,819	+6,779
Black Population Change from 1950-1970	+2106	+7,464	+2,749	+7,472	+8,890
Percent Black – 1970	96.26%	95.91%	97.15%	94.30%	
Percent Black – 1960	56.54%	5.09%	92.57%	11.67%	
Percent Black – 1950	00.17%	0.13%	0.50%	0.05%	
Population Under Age 14 – 1970	506	2,674	702	2,715	2,511
Population Age 25 and Over – 1970	1,282	3,422	1,560	3,653	5,134
% Population Under 14 – 1970	23.08%	34.32%	24.70%	34.25%	26.89%
% Adults 25 Years of Age and Older – 1970	58.49%	43.92%	54.89%	46.08%	54.98%
Ratio of Adults Age 25 and over to Children under Age 14 – 1970	2.53	1.28	2.22	1.35	2.04

% of Population Age 14 and over married not widowed, living apart or divorced	59.19%	56.79%	58.69%	58.83%	64.85%
% of Children under 18 Living with Both Parents	61.09%	53.90%	63.16%	61.40%	70.37%
% of Children under 18 Living with Mother Alone	24.47%	27.54%	17.55%	25.79%	15.20%
% Completed College	7.18%	1.55%	15.45%	4.38%	19.56%
% Never to Have Attended HS	29.72%	44.86%	25.71%	40.08%	19.93%
% Men Age 14 and over employed	80.39%	73.84%	79.13%	73.30%	80.35%
% Females Age 14 and over employed	63.69%	54.98%	61.57%	56.28%	60.62%
% White Collar Employed	39.36%	28.15%	51.05%	32.14%	55.03%
% Skilled Blue Collar Employed	33.03%	33.76%	24.36%	36.61%	24.39%
% Unskilled Blue Collar Employed	27.59%	37.53%	24.58%	31.09%	20.34%
% Population in Lowest Three Income Segments	11.75%	11.75%	6.93%	12.24%	6.82%
% Population in the Three Highest Income Segments	20.27%	20.27%	30.30%	10.95%	29.59%
Median Family Income	$8,663	$7,303	$11,461	$8.724	$10,431
Median Home Value – Owner Occupied	$11,700	$9,200	$11,400	$9,100	$14,200
Occupied Dwellings	765	1,972	838	2,086	2,916
% Occupied Dwellings Owner Occupied	35.42%	24.39%	61.34%	27.33%	56.96%
Renter Occupied Dwellings	494	1,491	324	1,516	1,255
Median Monthly Rent	$94	$108	$101	$110	$110

Table 7

Metric	15-0001	16-0001	18-0001	18-0002	16-0002	19-0001	16-0003
Population	5,194	6,128	2,399	3,140	5,777	4,465	3,951
Population Under Age 14	1,726	1,488	712	990	1,820	1,411	1,215
Population Age 25 and Over	2,548	3,591	1,278	2,189	2,799	2,189	1,910
% Population Under 14	33.23%	24.28%	29.68%	31.53%	31.50%	31.60%	30.75%
% Adults 25 Years of Age and Older	49.06%	58.60%	53.27%	69.71%	48.45%	49.03%	48.34%
Ratio of Adults Age 25 and over to Children under Age 14	1.36	2.41	1.79	2.21	1.54	1.55	1.57
% of Population Age 14 and over married not widowed, living apart or divorced	46.34%	49.76%	45.82%	47.58%	49.81%	50.56%	47.08%
% of Children under 18 Living with Both Parents	33.12%	40.18%	33.51%	42.60%	38.83%	39.15%	39.70%
% of Children under 18 Living with Mother Alone	50.45%	35.92%	43.78%	36.14%	37.76%	40.61%	42.27%
% Completed College	1.41%	2.90%	0.00%	0.55%	0.71%	0.55%	1.05%
% Never to Have Attended HS	59.93%	54.97%	73.00%	63.96%	60.91%	30.04%	49.06%
% Men Age 16 ad over employed	54.91%	54.19%	38.84%	53.59%	52.98%	48.58%	56.34%
% Females Age 16 and over employed	32.08%	38.14%	32.83%	32.15%	30.28%	33.95%	39.14%
% White Collar Employed	23.75%	24.94%	18.81%	23.50%	17.10%	30.04%	21.07%

% Skilled Blue Collar Employed	27.18%	31.31%	24.05%	33.18%	32.73%	52.19%	40.41%
% Unskilled Blue Collar Employed	48.35%	46.09%	56.06%	45.39%	49.83%	22.06%	43.68%
% Population in Lowest Three Income Segments	37.33%	27.16%	44.44%	30.65%	31.72%	29.27%	23.71%
% Population in the Three Highest Income Segments	5.05%	2.93%	0.00%	3.08%	5.10%	6.10%	6.74%
Median Family Income	$4,290	$5,450	$3,359	$5,211	$4,921	$5,558	$5,489
Median Home Value – Owner Occupied	$5,500	$6,400	$5,200	$6,000	$5,900	$5,400	$6,300
Occupied Dwellings	1,583	2,134	814	909	1,738	1,368	1,088
% Occupied Dwellings Owner Occupied	11.31%	17.20%	7.49%	11.55%	17.15%	11.92%	17.56%
Renter Occupied Dwellings	1,404	1,767	753	804	1,440	1,205	897
Median Monthly Rent	$63	$64	$55	$60	$67	$64	$73

The 5 sampled tracts that shifted racially from 1950 to 1970 also provide an insight about the demographic evolution of Cherry Hill. Their transformation is reflected by the analysis below.

Last, the several 1970 tracts occupying the same location as the original 1950 predominantly Black tracts are reflected in the analysis below.

During the 1960s, Cherry Hill's growth began to stabilize, slowing from a prodigious growth rate of 96.17% the preceding decade to a more modest rate of just 4.73%. However, social progress within Cherry Hill proved a more complex phenomenon to capture in numbers. Consider, on the one hand, that the ranks of those Cherry Hill families occupying the three highest income categories of the census expanded from just 5 in 1950 to 153 by 1960, a net growth of 148 families reflecting an expansion of more than 30 times over the decade. From 1960 to 1970, the numbers of families in the three highest income categories went from 153 to just 177, a more modest growth rate of 15.69%. During the same period, the number of families in the three lowest income categories moved from 475 (28.79%) in 1950, swelling to 1,054 (39.29%) by 1960, and then shrinking to 686 (22.76%) in 1970.

The number of people employed in unskilled blue collar positions expanded a small portion from 1,002 (51.9% of all employed) in 1950 to 1,156 in 1960. However, this growth in the workers falling within this segment of the labor force still represented only 45.59% of those employed in 1960. The unskilled blue collar sector again grew only slightly in 1970 to 1,285. However, this number represented an even smaller percentage of the employed at 24.65%.

Cherry Hill's core of skilled blue collar workers stabilized during the 1950s and 1960s. Workers filling these skilled occupations numbered 672 (34.91% of all employed) in 1950, 921 (36.32% of all employed) in 1960, and 1,556 (36.57% of all employed) in 1970.

It is the growth of workers within white collar occupations that would seem to promise social progress for the residents of Cherry Hill. In 1950, the persons employed within this segment of the work force numbered 251 (13.03% of the employed population) in 1950, 459 (18.09% of the employed) in 1960, and 1,372 (32.24% of the employed) in 1970.

Probing deeper into the numbers, this growth of a white-collar work-force in Cherry Hill appears not to reflect a new skill set borne out of a marked increase statistically in educational achievement or expanded work experience among residents. While the percentage of residents age 25 and older who never attended high school declined from 55.01% in 1950, to 49.31% in 1960, and continued to shrink to 40.88% in 1970, the percentage of residents completing college remained essentially the same. In 1950, the portion of this 25-year-and-older segment that completed college was 2.04%. In 1960, the percentage was just 2.45%, and by 1970, the percentage had risen slightly to only 3.61%.

Rather, the development that most accounts for the migration of Cherry Hill residents into white collar positions was the expansion of government employment in Baltimore.

Table 8

Work Force Indicators	Baltimore	2502.01	2502.02	2502.03	2502.04	Cherry Hill
Government Workers – 1950	37,142					255
Percent of Work Force – 1950	9.49%					12.79%
Government Workers – 1960	43,554					436
Percent of Workforce – 1960	12.02%					14.14%
Government Workers – 1970	70,804	192	63	375	507	1,137
Percent of Workforce – 1970	20.08%	32.93%	12.68%	23.75%	31.77%	26.72%
Private Wage and Salary – 1950	321,494					1,693
Percent of Workforce – 1950	82.12%					84.90%
Private Wage and Salary – 1960	294,704					2,617
Percent of Workforce – 1960	81.34%					84.86%
Private Wage and Salary – 1970	267,744	391	430	1,106	1,065	2,992

(Continued)

Table 8 – *Continued*

Work Force Indicators	Baltimore	2502.01	2502.02	2502.03	2502.04	Cherry Hill
Percent of Workforce – 1970	75.93%	67.07%	86.52%	70.04%	66.73%	70.32%
Self-Employed Workers – 1950	31,693					46
Percent of Workforce – 1950	8.10%					2.31%
Self-Employed Workers – 1960	22,328					31
Percent of Workforce – 1960	6.16%					1.01%
Self-Employed Workers – 1970	13,385	0	4	98	24	126
Percent of Workforce- 1970	3.80%	0.00%	0.80%	6.21%	1.50%	2.96%
Unpaid Family Workers – 1950	1,158					0
Percent of Workforce – 1950	0.30%					0.00%
Unpaid Family Workers – 1960	1,725					0
Percent of Workforce – 1960	0.48%					0.00%
Unpaid Family Workers – 1970	767	0	0	0	0	0
Percent of Workforce – 1970	0.22%	0.00%	0.00%	0.00%	0.00%	0.00%

The above table reflects the emergence of the government sector as a prevailing source of employment in Cherry Hill, and particularly in that most populous Cherry Hill Census Tract, 2502.04, at a rate greater than is reflected in the City at large. In addition, the 1970 Census associates with that source of employment an expansion of clerical employment throughout the several Cherry Hill Census Tracts, including that most populous one.

Nonetheless, social progress within Cherry Hill was neither uniform nor simple from 1960 to 1970. One area challenging any simple explanation of social progress involves wealth creation in the form of home ownership. In 1950, Cherry Hill possessed 484 owner-occupied dwellings out of a total of 1,575 occupied units, accounting for a rate of home ownership of 30.73%. In 1960, out of an explosion of 2,822 occupied dwellings, an increase of 79.17%, Cherry Hill had just 669 owner-occupied dwellings, a declining ownership rate of 23.71%. This prodigious increase in housing units saw an overall *decrease* in the percentage of owned dwellings. That pattern continued over the next ten years. Out of 3,581 occupied dwellings, an increase of an additional 759 occupied units from 1970 (an increase of still 26.90%), owners occupied just 568 – a net loss of 101 owner-occupied dwellings from 1960.

The numbers tell us that Cherry Hill was losing home owners at least from 1960 through 1970 while it was accumulating a growing population of renters. At the time, Cherry Hill enjoyed a relatively stagnant or declining rate of home ownership, a very different result is evidenced by the racially transitioning census tracts in this analysis – Coppin Heights/ Mondawmin, Hanlon Park, Lower Greenspring, Lower Park Heights, and Ashburton.

The demographics of these transitioning tracts reveal shifts from what were upscale white collar predominantly White communities to predominantly Black communities within 10-to-20 years. In this transition, the emerging predominantly Black communities developed in varying ways to sustain or to abandon the prior established patterns of home ownership in these tracts. The differing experiences of these communities are reflected in the table below.

While the evolving all-Black communities in Hanlon Park and Ashburton showed a decline in home ownership, the decline was not substantial. On the other hand, the communities in Coppin Heights/ Mondawmin, Lower Greenspring, and Lower Park Heights experienced substantial reductions in home ownership previously known by their near all-White predecessors. Even these latter census tracts sustained home ownership at a more substantial rate than any of the Cherry Hill tracts.

Consequently, during the 1960s, Black families within these transitioning census tracts advanced to home ownership as ownership within the Cherry Hill tracts was becoming less common than it had been during the

Table 9

Metric	Coppin Heights-Mondawmin	Lower Greenspring	Hanlon Park	Lower Park Heights	Ashburton
Occupied Dwellings – 1950	753	1,914	753	1,916	2,606
Occupied Dwellings – 1960	613	1,907	835	1,817	2,538
Change in Occupied Dwellings from 1950 to 1960	-140	-7	+82	-99	-68
Percent Change in Occupied Dwellings 1950-1960	-18.59%	0.37%	10.90%	5.17%	2.59%
Occupied Dwellings – 1970	765	1,972	838	2,086	2,916
Change in Occupied Dwellings from 1960 to 1970	+152	+65	+3	+262	+378
Percent Change in Occupied Dwellings 1960-1970	24.80%	3.41%	0.36%	14.42%	14.89%
Owner Occupied – 1950	368	1,304	512	1,319	1,645
Owner Occupied – 1960	329	1,122	558	1,185	1,629
Change in Owner-Occupied Dwellings from 1950 to 1960	-39	-182	+46	-134	-16
Percent Change in Owner-Occupied Dwellings 1950-1960	-10.60%	-13.96%	+8.98%	-10.16%	0.97%
Owner Occupied – 1970	271	481	514	570	1,661
Change in Owner-Occupied Dwellings from 1960 to 1970	-58	-641	-44	-615	+32
Percent Change in Owner-Occupied Dwellings 1960-1970	-21.40%	-57.13%	-7.88%	-51.90%	+1.96%
Percent Owner Occupied – 1950	50.20%	68.13%	67.99%	68.84%	63.12%
Percent Owner Occupied – 1960	53.67%	58.84%	66.83%	65.22%	64.18%
Percent Owner Occupied – 1970	35.42%	24.39%	61.34%	27.33%	56.96%

Linda G. Morris

1950s. The transitioning tracts gained Black home owners while Cherry Hill was losing them.

Considering the variation of more traditional social progress indicators demonstrated within the Cherry Hill Tracts and among the transitioning predominantly Black tracts, reliable expectations of sustainable success for these communities remained complex. Home ownership rates differed across the board for these tracts, and statistics for educational attainment ranged both high and low. Still, for the transitioning tracts, data on employment for the male population age 16 and older remained well above 70% and, in some cases, beyond 80%, largely consistent with rates sustained for the predecessor predominantly White populations.

The employment data for males in the Cherry Hill tracks clung on at just above 70%. As noted, the population in Cherry Hill's three lowest income categories declined during the 1960s, as did the work force of unskilled blue collar workers. Yet, the profile in Cherry Hill presented a number of troubling signs for the future. For much of the 1950s, and into the 1960s, Cherry Hill had enjoyed among the highest percentage of young people under 18 living with both parents. In the 1970 census, the percentage had moved from 72.44% in 1960 to 43.20% in just 10 years. Indeed, the percentage of children living with two parents in populous Cherry Hill Tract 2502.04 was as low as 29.66%.

Placed in its statistical context, the 43.20% of children under 18 living with both parents is particularly troubling considering that the Cherry Hill tracts, particularly Tract 2502.04, had the largest population under 14 relative to the population age 25 and over.[11] From 1950 through 1970, Cherry Hill was a community of a growing population of children overseen by a shrinking population of adults. From 1950 through 1960, Cherry Hill seemed to blossom as a place of growing families.

However, as Cherry Hill moved beyond 1970, the following questions loomed. Would this arrangement continue with fewer and fewer adults rearing more and more children? Would the arrangement continue to be sustainable indefinitely? If not, for how much longer would allow Cherry Hill to remain what it once was?

A Demographic Epilogue

According to a 2011 Baltimore City Health Department Neighborhood Health Profile for Cherry Hill,[12] the above noted family arrangement reflected in the Census data for 1950, 1960, and 1970 continued to the present. More and more of Cherry Hill's children came to be reared by fewer and fewer adults.

In 2010, Baltimore's population had fallen to 616,802,[13] a decline of 31.90% from 1970's 905,759. Cherry Hill's numbers had dropped to 8,202,[14] 42.10% of Cherry Hill's 1970 population of 14,166. In 2010, 35.7% of its population comprised children under 18.[15]

The 2011 Neighborhood Profile revealed that Cherry Hill's median household income was $19,193 compared to a median income for Baltimore City of $37,395.[16] In 2011, the reported median household income for Cherry Hill was 51.32% that for Baltimore City. In 1970, by contrast, Cherry Hill's mean income of $7,018[17] was 69.93% of the mean income for Baltimore City of $10,035.

The 2011 Profile reflects that the percentage of the population in Cherry Hill age 25 or older to have completed college was just 6.8%.[18] Just 40 years before, the 1970 Census reflected that 3.61% of that population had a college degree. Under the 2011 Profile statistics, the 6.8% figure translates in absolute terms to 291 people with a college degree. Under the reported figures for 1970, the identified population with a college degree comprised 178 people, just 113 fewer people than the total to arise 40 years thereafter.

While the 2011 Neighborhood Health Profile for Cherry Hill does not relate current housing data to the analysis here developed in terms of housing occupancy and home ownership,[19] the American Community Survey for 2011-2015 does. In 2015, Cherry Hill is reported as having 3,126 occupied units, of which only 403 were owner occupied, giving a rate of home ownership of 12.89%. The 1970 Census reported 568 dwellings owned by its occupants, reflecting a loss of 165 owner-occupied dwellings since that time. The 1970 rate of home ownership among the occupied dwellings was 15.86%.

By any analysis, the picture painted by the 2011 Neighborhood Profile and the 2011-2015 American Community Survey is not the reflection of social promise embodied by the census analyses from 1950, 1960, and even 1970. What happened to the promise of 65, 55, and even 45 years ago?

This demographic analysis supports several obvious observations. First, the Cherry Hill of the late 1940s and early 1950s was built in a way that accommodated the promise of the generations of veterans who had left to defend a nation that despised them and returned to claim the life's reward their sacrifice had earned.[20] Whether or not anyone intended it, the early Cherry Hill gave space for growth both physically and socially. Within in that space, the early occupants of Cherry Hill did indeed grow both socially and in numbers.

Linda G. Morris

The population exploded, nearly doubling between 1950 and 1960. The returning veterans apparently coming to Cherry Hill with skills that Black men in other all-Black enclaves of Baltimore did not possess formed in the 1950s a core of skilled blue-collar workers who sustained an expansion of home ownership by 1960, an advancement into the top three income categories, and a movement educationally to increase only incrementally the number of those with a college degree, and to expand the number of home owners.

The achievement of early Cherry Hill residents was, however, blunted by the housing decisions of the planners who had conceived Cherry Hill when they chose to expand Cherry Hill not from this middle core of skilled blue collar workers but by expanding the poorest segments of Cherry Hill's population. Even with that expansion, Cherry Hill was resilient in its capacity to sustain growth by moving people from the bottom three income segments. From 1950 to 1970, the ranks of the population in the three lowest income segments declined, as Cherry Hill's population expanded.

Ultimately, Cherry Hill was built to accommodate human need, not to promote human growth. Perhaps, those who planned Cherry Hill had difficulty seeing the promise that drove those original returning World War II veterans. In the space that Cherry Hill's first residents found there to pursue their aspirations, the planners found ample space *only* for rental housing, together with subsidized housing for the poorest ranks of the Black community. These planners developed little housing for ownership to meet the prevailing expectations for social progress and rising aspirations among Cherry Hill's own residents. In a community that initially sustained rising expectations among people not expecting to have or to meet expectations, the community ironically was not built to satisfy such expectations. To fulfill a destiny that they determined, these aspiring families had to leave Cherry Hill. And many such families did leave, seeking out better lives in those transitioning communities like the evolving all-Black communities in tracts like Coppin Height/Mondawmin, Hanlon Park, Lower Greenspring, Lower Park Heights, and maybe Ashburton. But not Cherry Hill.

In the end, Cherry Hill had room only for need and neediness – not for otherwise unexpected and unfulfilled promise. To this extent, Cherry Hill represents a lost opportunity. For those fortunate enough to have lived there during those early years, it was a lost dream not only of what was, but also of what could have been.

THE END

1

Tract - 1950	Associated Neighborhood
25-02A	**CHERRY HILL**
1-2	**Upper Canton** – *Working class largely White Ethnic East Baltimore community a few blocks off the eastern harbor.*
1-3	**Patterson Park** – *Working class largely White ethnic community in the neighborhoods immediately surrounding Patterson Park.*
12-1	**Lower Roland Park** – *Upper class white collar community north of the Homewood campus of Johns Hopkins University.*
12-2	**Guilford** – *Upper class community immediately east and south of Homewood campus of Johns Hopkins University*
15-1	**Sandtown-Winchester** – *Tract immediately southwest of the intersection where the Freddie Gray unrest was centered in April 2015.*
15-5	**Coppin Heights/Mondawmin** – *Tract in West Baltimore including the area immediately surrounding Coppin State University and Mondawmin Mall*
15-7A	**Hanlon Park** – *Tract in Northwest Baltimore surrounding reservoir off Liberty Heights and Gwynn Falls Parkway.*
15-11	**Ashburton** – *Tract North of Liberty Heights Avenue in Northwest Baltimore that includes the upper-class community of largely individual homes*
15-12	**Lower Greenspring** – *Tract just northwest of Druid Hill Park surrounding Children's Hospital*
15-13	**Lower Park Heights** – *Tract in Northwest Baltimore north of the light rail line west of thee Lower Greenspring Tract, largely south of Reisterstown Road.*
16-1	**Lower Sandtown** – *Portion of Sandtown-Winchester community west of Carey Street, north of Edmondson Avenue, west of Fremont, south of Laurens*
16-2	**Middle Sandtown** – *Portion of Sandtown community south of Laurens, north of Edmondson, east of Gilmore, and west of Carey*
16-3	**West Sandtown** – *Portion of Sandtown community north of Edmondson Avenue, south of Laurens, east of Fulton, and west of Gilmore*
26-10	**Upper Highlandtown** – *East Baltimore working class community south of Monument Street, north of Bank Street, west of Highland, east of Conkling*
26-11	**Lower Highlandtown** – *East Baltimore working class community south of Bank Street, west of Highland, north of Toone, east of Conkling*

(Continued)

Tract - 1950	Associated Neighborhood
27-11	**Lower Homeland** – *Upper class North Baltimore community west of York Road, east of the Light Rail Line, north of Cold Spring Land, and South of Homeland*
27-12	**Upper Homeland** – *Upper class North Baltimore community west of York Road, east of the Light Rail Line, north of Homeland, and south of the City Line*

2 The incomes for the sampled tracts from Table 1 (median household income) and Table 3 of the 1950 Census for Baltimore City reflect the following ranking of the sampled tracts (the tracts in bold are the predominantly Black tracts.

	Median Household Income (1949 Dollars)	Median Home Value (1949 Dollars)
Upper Homeland	**$6,947.00**	$20,000
Lower Roland Park	**$5,412.00**	$20,000.00
Ashburton	**$5,080.00**	$13,990.00
Hanlon Park	**$4,250.00**	$10,626.00
Coppin /Mondawmin	**$4,083.00**	$9,885.00
Lower Homeland	**$3,639.00**	$16,695.00
Lower Park Heights	**$3,597.00**	$7,434.00
Lower Highlandtown	**$3,485.00**	$5,905.00
Lower Greenspring	**$3,387.00**	$8,236.00
Upper Canton	**$3,375.00**	$6,795.00
Upper Highlandtown	**$3,360.00**	$6,358.00
Patterson Park	**$2,992.00**	$5,099.00
Baltimore City	**$2,817.00**	$7,113.00
Guilford	**$2,765.00**	$10,389.00
Cherry Hill	**$2,239.00**	$6,443.00
West Sandtown	**$2,042.00**	$6,008.00
Sandtown/Winchester	**$1,890.00**	$5,157.00
Middle Sandtown	**$1,791.00**	$5,336.00
Lower Sandtown	**$1,707.00**	$6,338.00

3 The Table below computed from 1950 Table 2 for the sampled tracts, showing the percentage of males, females, and all persons age 14 and over counted as employed.

	% Employed	% Female	% Male
West Sandtown	58.60%	44.41%	74.50%
Lower Sandtown	58.32%	46.07%	72.17%
Lower Highlandtown	57.49%	34.73%	76.92%
Middle Sandtown	56.24%	42.87%	71.52%
Hanlon Park	56.11%	30.41%	85.51%
Upper Canton	55.26%	32.32%	79.44%
Patterson Park	54.50%	32.82%	76.11%
Upper Highlandtown	53.87%	29.05%	79.56%
Baltimore City	53.19%	33.05%	75.01%
Ashburton	53.10%	23.77%	85.59%
SandtownWinchester	52.54%	36.97%	68.22%
Lower Greenspring	52.23%	29.26%	78.28%
Lower Park Heights	51.69%	27.84%	77.74%
Guilford	51.42%	41.45%	65.53%
Lower Ashburton	51.24%	27.10%	80.15%
Cherry Hill	48.67%	26.38%	73.45%
Lower Homeland	47.53%	26.64%	76.38%
Upper Homeland	47.27%	22.63%	76.27%

4 The Table below drawn from Table 1 of the 1950 Census, reflects the percentage of households counted fall within the three lowest and three highest income segments reported in the table.

	% Three Lowest Income Segments	% Three Highest Income Segments
Lower Sandtown	45.10%	2.65%
Middle Sandtown	41.62%	1.98%
Sandtown	38.77%	2.11%
West Sandtown	37.04%	3.95%
Guilford	32.18%	17.42%
Lower Homeland	29.23%	34.87%

(Continued)

	% Three Lowest Income Segments	% Three Highest Income Segments
Cherry Hill	28.79%	0.30%
Baltimore City	26.19%	11.38%
Patterson Park	20.23%	8.95%
Lower Greenspring	19.15%	15.96%
Lower Ashburton	17.61%	23.24%
Upper Canton	17.10%	12.17%
Roland Park	15.20%	46.00%
Upper Homeland	15.09%	55.66%
Lower Park Heights	14.18%	15.38%
Hanlon Park	14.04%	24.45%
Lower Highlandtown	13.27%	11.95%
Upper Highlandtown	13.06%	10.98%
Ashburton	10.63%	36.23%

5 The table below reflects the percentage of skilled blue collar workers, "Craftsmen" and "Operatives and Kindred Workers" among the population 14 and over counted as employed.

	% Skilled Blue Collar
Patterson Park	54.82%
Upper Highlandtown	52.59%
Lower Highlandtown	50.36%
Upper Canton	47.46%
Baltimore City	35.77%
Cherry Hill	34.91%
West Sandtown	31.31%
Sandtown	26.96%
Lower Park Heights	26.46%
Middle Sandtown	23.62%
Lower Greenspring	23.05%
Hanlon Park	16.51%
Lower Homeland	12.24%
Upper Homeland	11.03%

(Continued)

	% Skilled Blue Collar
Guilford	10.43%
Lower Sandtown	9.39%
Ashburton Coppin	9.21%
Heights/Mondawmin	9.20%
Roland Park	3.78%

6 The table below reflects the percentage of households comprising married couples with their own household noted in Table 1 of the 1950 Census for Baltimore.

	% Households Married Couples with own Households
Lower Park Heights	93.22%
Cherry Hill	83.70%
Upper Highlandtown	83.39%
Ashburton	83.37%
Hanlon Park	83.22%
Lower Greenspring	82.41%
Upper Homeland	79.95%
Lower Homeland	79.71%
Upper Canton	78.98%
Lower Highlandtown Coppin	78.85%
Heights/Mondawmin	76.82%
West Sandtown	72.61%
Baltimore City	72.09%
Patterson Park	71.59%
Sandtown	64.69%
Middle Sandtown	62.10%
Lower Sandtown	54.79%
Roland Park	54.22%
Guilford	51.88%

7 The Table below is drawn from Table 1 of the 1950 Census and Table P-1 of the 1960 Census.

	1950	1960	% Change	Black Pop-1950	Black Pop- 1960	% Black Pop Change	% Black 1960
Baltimore City	949,706	939,024	-1.12%	225,099	325,589	44.64%	34.67%
Cherry Hill	6,895	13,526	96.17%	6,845	13,506	97.31%	99.85%
Upper Canton	5,675	5,103	-10.08%	0	0	0.00%	0.00%
Patterson Park	4,604	3,822	-16.99%	3	0	-100.00%	0.00%
Lower Roland Park	3,495	3,495	0.00%	52	30	-42.31%	0.86%
Guilford	7,446	7,499	0.71%	359	226	-37.05%	3.01%
Sandtown-Winchester Coppin	9,470	7,373	-22.14%	9,263	7,324	-20.93%	99.34%
Heights/Mondawmin	2,294	2,064	-10.03%	4	1,167	29075.00%	56.54%
Hanlon Park	2,409	2,944	22.21%	12	2,737	22708.33%	92.97%
Ashburton	8,391	7,677	-8.51%	22	2,133	9595.45%	27.78%
Lower Greenspring	6,284	6,091	-3.07%	8	310	3775.00%	5.09%
Lower Park Heights	6,433	5,623	-12.59%	3	656	21766.67%	11.67%
Lower Sandtown	6,937	5,320	-23.31%	6,880	5,295	-23.04%	99.53%
Middle Sandtown	8,902	6,126	-31.18%	8,859	6,091	-31.25%	99.43%
West Sandtown	5,863	4,575	-21.97%	5,786	4,560	-21.19%	99.67%
Upper Highlandtown	5,313	4,365	-17.84%	3	2	-33.33%	0.05%
Lower Highlandtown	4,066	3,567	-12.27%	1	4	300.00%	0.11%
Lower Homeland	2,810	2,786	-0.85%	45	15	-66.67%	0.54%
Upper Homeland	6,069	6,648	9.54%	165	139	-15.76%	2.09%

8 The data supporting the above paragraph and the Table that follows is drawn from Table 3 of the 1950 Census for Baltimore and Tables H-1 and H-2 of the 1960 Census.

9 The data from the table below was drawn from Table P-1 of the 1960 Census.

	% under 18 living with both parents
Baltimore City	77.03%
Cherry Hill	72.44%
Upper Canton	80.26%
Patterson Park	86.07%
Roland Park	81.63%
Guilford	67.62%
Sandtown	49.50%
Coppin Heights/Mondawmin	75.52%
Hanlon Park	78.10%
Ashburton	87.80%
Lower Greenspring	83.39%
Lower Park Heights	86.00%
Lower Sandtown	57.35%
Middle Sandtown	50.78%
West Sandtown	55.83%
Upper Highlandtown	83.09%
Lower Highlandtown	87.95%
Lower Homeland	91.84%
Upper Homeland	90.13%

10 The several census tracts making up Cherry Hill in the 1970 Census consisted of the following designated areas:

1. **Tract 2502.01:** The area east of the railroad tracks, now light rail line, that intersected Waterview Avenue, connecting in a straight line to Cherry Hill Road, several blocks west of Berea Road, and proceeding along Cherry Hill Road to Round Road (moving north), which street proceeding to the water, crossing Waterview Avenue, formed

the eastern boundary of the tract. This tract is the western most of the tracts closest to Westport and downtown Baltimore.

2. **Tract 2502.02:** The tract immediately east of Tract 2502.01, bound on the west by Round Road, completing the western boundary, and then proceeding along Cherry Hill Road to the intersection of Round Rd, on the south by Joplea Avenue, proceeding to its intersection with Joseph Avenue southeast to its intersection with Cherry Hill Road, forming the eastern boundary of the tract to Potee Avenue, which, proceeded to the Hanover Street Bridge and the water to complete the eastern boundary. The Middle Branch bounds this tract on the north.

3. **Tract 2502.03:** The tract immediately east of Tract 2502.02, bound on the west by the combination of Cherry Hill Road and Potee Avenue, with the Middle Branch forming its northern boundary. The tract was bounded on the South by Cherryland Road, proceeding east to Reedbird Avenue, completing its eastern boundary of the tract at the water.

4. **Tract 2502.04:** This tract is immediately south of the above three tracts, bounded to its south by the old B & O rail line, now light rail line, on the west by the same straight line boundary of Tract 2501.01, proceeding northeast from the light rail line to connect with Cherry Hill Road, several blocks west of Berea Road. The tract was therefore south of Cherry Hill Road to where it connects with Round Road. The expanse of the tract was then east of Round Road where Round Road connected with Joplea Avenue, which formed the northern boundary of the tract until Joplea Avenue reached Joseph Avenue, proceeding Southeast until it connected with Cherry Hill Road, proceeding southwest until that road connected with Cherryland Road, which completed the northern boundary of the tract until it reached Reedbird Avenue, forming the eastern boundary until Reedbird Avenue completed the circuit, reaching the southern boundary of the light rail tracks.

11 The ratio of adults age 25 and older to children under 14 for all the Cherry Hill Census Tracts is 0.83 for 1970, improved from 0.69 for 1960. That ratio for 1970 should be qualified by information placing the ratio for Tract 2502.04 at 0.58, with the 63.53% of children under 18 living with a single mother. That statistic represents a new trend for Cherry Hill.

12 Ames, A., Evans, M., Fox, L., Milam, A., Petteway, R., Rutledge, R.. *2011 Neighborhood Health Profile: Cherry Hill*. Baltimore City Health

Department, December 2011. Digitally available at http://www. baltimorehealth.org/dataresearch.html.

13 Ames, A., etc., *2011 Neighborhood Health Profile Cherry Hill*, at p. 3.

14 *Id.*

15 *Id.* In 1970, 48.36% of the Cherry Hill was under age 18.

16 *Id.* at p. 4.

17 Because the 1970 census offered no aggregated data for Cherry Hill as a community, rather than data within 4 census tracts, each reported median associated only with its respective tract, this data is not capable of being aggregated. The 1970 census did, however, give a data estimate for the mean, or average, income for each of the four tracts, in addition to a median figure, the point where half of the population was above and the other half below. The mean given for each tract, together with the report of the number of families reporting for each tract, therefore, allows for this data to be aggregated for all four tracts and then processed to provide a mean or average income for all four tracts.

18 Ames, A., etc., *2011 Neighborhood Health Profile Cherry Hill*, at p. 5.

19 The housing data from the 2011 Neighborhood Health Profile for Cherry Hill does not reflect the housing occupancy data used for this demographic analysis. Table DP04 from the American Community Survey for 2011-2015 contains the most recent data on housing occupancy within the current tracts that occupy the same geography as those tracts used from the 1950, 1960, and 1970 Census. The 2010 tracts for Cherry Hill include Tract 2502.03, 2502.04, and 2502.07.

20 This is *not* to say that Cherry Hill was designed to promote the highest aspirations of these returning Black veterans of World War II. Rather, the people who conceived Cherry Hill quite clearly intended to build a community where the returning Black veteran would live their lives with their families out of sight and out of mind. That the community that the veterans came to create exceeded anyone's expectations but their own may have been only an unintended consequence of the isolation and the open space associated with the early days of that development.

Acknowledgments

I want to acknowledge the following persons and organizations without whose assistance this story could not have been documented and shared with you:

Baltimore Archdiocese

Baltimore City Health Department

Dr. John Breihan, Professor Emeritus, Loyola University of Maryland

Dennis C. Curry, Chief Archeologist, Maryland Historical Trust

Amanda Hughes, Maryland Department, Enoch Pratt Free Library

Father Frank Hull and Carla Canady, Josephite Seminary Archives

Michael K. Jackson, Manager, Special Collections, Enoch Pratt Free Library

Paul McCardell, Librarian, The Baltimore Sun

Sharon Morris, M.L.S., Director, DC Regional Libraries, Johns Hopkins University

Sally A. Robinson, Senior Counsel, Office of Legal Counsel, Baltimore City Public Schools

Magdelena Rudnicka, Baltimore City Housing Authority

Dale W. Shelton, Maryland Geological Survey, Maryland Department of Natural Resources

Timothy J. Thomas, Senior Vice President, Business Development, The Baltimore Sun

and

All of you in the first generation of Cherry Hill children who have worked with me to bring our story to life. You know who you are!